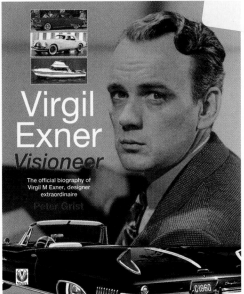

Virgil Exner
Visioneer

The official biography of
Virgil M Exner, designer
extraordinaire

Peter Grist

For post production news, updates and amendments relating to this book please visit www.veloce.co.uk/V4863

www.veloce.co.uk

First published in August 2007 by Veloce Publishing Limited, Veloce House, Parkway Farm Business Park, Middle Farm Way, Poundbury, Dorchester DT1 3AR, England. Fax 01305 268864 / e-mail info@veloce.co.uk / web www.veloce.co.uk or www.velocebooks.com. New edition published September 2015 ISBN: 978-1-845848-63-7 UPC: 6-36847-04863-1

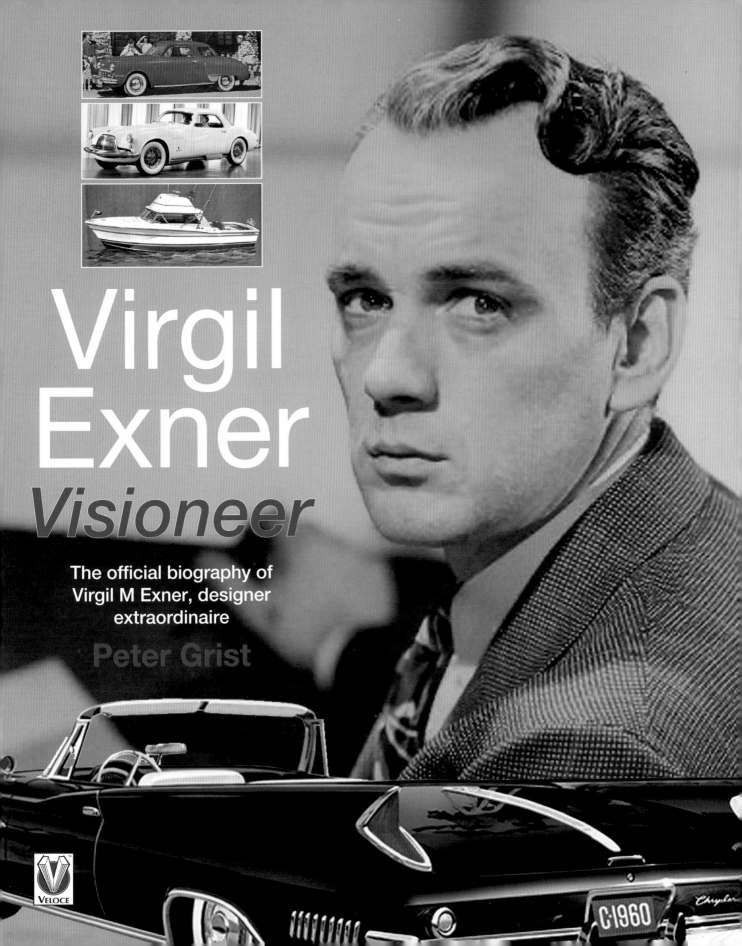

Virgil
Exner
Visioneer

The official biography of
Virgil M Exner, designer
extraordinaire

Peter Grist

VELOCE

CONTENTS

INTRODUCTION

Virgil Exner's influence on my life has been huge. From my teenage years came a passion for 1950s rock 'n' roll, and from that stemmed a greater passion for the cars of that era, the best of which, in my opinion, were the offerings from the Chrysler Corporation. To eventually own an example (a 1959 De Soto) was a dream come true, and led me to create a club for fellow enthusiasts in the UK and Europe. Running that club and editing its magazine, *TalkFlite*, gave me the opportunity to meet many of Exner's fans around the world and to get into motoring journalism writing for other magazines and internet sites. Almost all of these articles, and the books I have written, have featured Exner's designs somewhere along the way, so I have a lot to thank him for. It is unfortunate that he is predominantly remembered for his finned cars alone, as his work and legacy to the automotive world was so much more than that.

I was honored and flattered when I was asked to write his biography, and although it has been a labor of love, I have strived to make it as unbiased as possible. I could not have achieved this task without the unfaltering support of Virgil Exner Jr, whose encyclopaedic mind was a mine of critical information. I hope you will enjoy the journey of discovery into Exner's life, be amazed at his artistic talent, be inspired by his work ethic and vision, and comforted by the wealth and richness of his legacy to all of us: the countless classic cars and boats we own or dream of owning.

Peter Grist

FOREWORD

My parents were caring, family oriented, hard-working, responsible, and small town Michigan people who were brought up the same way. They were rather shy, but confident and resourceful, both having attended two years of college. Mom was a farm girl who was good at accounting, homemaking, and a pert, good-looking redhead. Father was 'Hollywood' handsome, athletically built, and especially good at art. We were a close family, including my younger sisters, Bronwen and Marie. The whole family loved sports, particularly auto-racing. Mother and father both had a good sense of humor, but father

could never tell a corny joke straight, which was funny in itself. He was usually quiet, serious, and soft spoken. We always preferred free time at home or going fishing to socializing, and home cooking to stepping out, but we all loved to travel.

Father's mechanical aptitude was greatly encouraged by my grandfather, and both loved automobile racing. My grandmother encouraged his natural artistic ability. With little formal training, he excelled in music, drawing, painting, and sculpture. He was very adept at transparent watercolor, but could handle most all mediums with great skill. It led to his design conviction as to how things ought to look, automobiles in particular. They should exude forward motion and function with simple, clean, sculptural elegance that relies on design continuity to present a 'whole' picture of curb appealing beauty. He always maintained there was "good art and bad art, and good design and bad design". His design integrity and style may easily be traced from a small sketch, through his paintings, to any one of his car designs. He was determined, patient, and persistent in pursuing his transportation design career.

Father was really a 'romantic' at heart. He loved the Wild West, collected guns, a few swords, and Joan of Arc art. He liked to read about Civil War battles, good historical novels, ship sinking mysteries, Knights of the Round Table, and castles. His own favorite contemporary artists were Russell Flint, Rockwell Kent, and N C Wyeth.

Father's last artwork was to be a series of paintings that depicted great castles of Europe. He was deeply researching the subject and had made beautiful color concept sketches for them. Of course he also loved "God, country, and Notre Dame".

Mother had her complexities and father his foibles, but they always confided in each other and me. I heard father tell Mom twice: "Hon, I have to start all over again." One was when he came home from Chrysler after seeing his 'Styling Section' for the first time. The other was when he was replaced at Chrysler in 1962. I'm sure he would have told her the same again, upon seeing the new Chrysler 300 of 2004.

I was, happily, brought up being encouraged to follow in father's footsteps, from his roaring sounds while making little race car sketches for me, to our building models together, and through our always close design relationship. Mom was the glue that bound us all, but father was my best friend, greatest mentor, and my inspirational hero.

I thank Peter Grist for his great integrity, persistence, and resourcefulness over the past few years in gathering the sometimes difficult to find and get material used in authoring this tome. Peter has the "gasoline in his blood" that father always talked about. I also greatly appreciate the input and cooperation of all those who aided Peter, and thank my dear wife Jan, who provided a lot of insight for me towards this endeavour.

Virgil M Exner Jr

July 1956. They stood beside the hospital bed, looking at the prone body. It appeared almost lifeless but for the constant low beep from the monitors. Virgil Exner stirred and became aware of the visitors standing close by and turned his ashen face towards them.

Mildred, his wife, and Tex Colbert, head of Chrysler Corporation looked worried. How could they possibly tell him that his latest concept car was lying at the bottom of the sea in the hull of a shipwrecked Italian liner, just days after he had undergone open heart surgery following a massive coronary?

The dry laugh that escaped from Exner's lips was not the response the gathered group had expected once they finally broached the subject.

Far from being upset, Chrysler's Vice President of Design realized that the car would become seafaring folklore, of which he was an enthusiast. Far better that than the unceremonious destruction that awaited the Norseman had it arrived at Chrysler's testing grounds.

For Jack and Molly Grist

1 "WITH SUCH A PENCIL, SUCH A PEN"

Virgil William Anderson was born at the University of Michigan Hospital in Ann Arbor, Michigan on 24th September 1909, to an unmarried 20-year-old by the name of Alvina Anderson. Alvina hailed from the farming community of Sturgeon Bay, Wisconsin, but was working as a housemaid in Escanaba, Michigan. Although there is little known about Exner's biological parents, Miss Anderson was known to be of Norwegian descent and Mr William Little, the father, was a 28-year-old Scottish-bred travelling agent from Iron River, Michigan. It was they who named the young boy Virgil William, presumably after the Roman poet Publius Vergilius Maro, better known today as Virgil. Official papers state that there were no supportive parents and poverty was the reason for his being placed in an adoption home, but one can assume that the social stigma at that time would be reason enough to have a child adopted, let alone other personal or financial considerations. The newborn child was placed into the care of The Michigan Children's Home Society under the general care of Mr Washington Gardner, then president of that organization. Virgil's luck soon changed for the better when Iva S and George W Exner, of Buchanan, Michigan, agreed to foster him. Eighteen months later, they finalized all the necessary paperwork and on 31st March 1911, Virgil William Anderson became Virgil Max Exner.

In 1891, Michigan had become the first state to require that a judge be satisfied as to the suitability of people who adopted, therefore George and Iva, who were unable to have their own children, would have fulfilled all the criteria as parents for Virgil, proving to be of 'good moral character' and showing their ability to support and educate the young boy in a suitable home. George's forebears hailed from northern Germany around the time of the American Civil War. He had little time for organized religion and preferred to spend his time with more productive and practical things. Iva was descended from Pennsylvania Dutch settlers and was a strict Mormon.

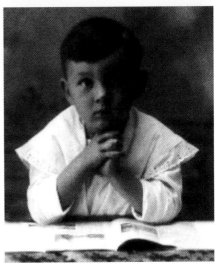

1913. Dreamer.

1911. The earliest known surviving picture of Virgil Max Exner, age 2.

Buchanan was a small farming town in the western part of Michigan, lying just north-west of South Bend, Indiana. Other than fruit and conventional farm crops, the main source of employment was with the Clark Equipment Company, which, during the industrial revolution, had its headquarters in Buchanan. George Exner worked as a head machinist for Clarks, putting to use his considerable skills and cultivating his inventive and creative side. George was adept at all facets of shop making, including woodworking, metalwork and, of course, machining. The young Virgil was encouraged by George to learn the various disciplines of a workshop, but from a very early age it was apparent that Virgil had a natural ability and keen interest in both art and athletics. Iva concluded that art was a safer way to spend time, so it was her, more than George, who lead Virgil to develop his embryonic skills in fine arts and away from machine work and athletics. She also encouraged him to play the violin and, later, the accordion.

The Exner's lived on the west side of town at 206 West 3rd Street, in a house that George Exner built almost entirely alone, using a Sears & Roebuck lumber kit and plans that were shipped in from Chicago. This two-story building featured a full-width, columned porch, a kitchen,

This is Virgil with his cousin, Lucille Sutphen, in 1914. The photo was professionally made into a postcard, but was never used.

dining room, indoor lavatory, three bedrooms, bathroom, and even a basement. What's more, the house still stands today, testament to George's superior workmanship. This quiet, dusty, unpaved (until just after WWII) part of town was where the young Virgil would spend his formative years.

As with most little boys, he and his friends had a passion for cowboys and the Wild West, an interest that would stay with Virgil into his later years, but his main fascination soon became automobiles. Virgil pondered not just the aesthetics of these beautiful creations but also the mechanics that drove them. Whilst still in high school, he and his closest friend, Arthur 'Art' Allen, would occasionally train the ninety miles east to Chicago for the big motor shows. The young Exner was not only enthralled with the automobiles but also fascinated with the whole magnificence of the show.

One car in particular made a huge impression on the boy; at the 1920 Chicago Motor Show, Virgil and Art risked reprimand and sneaked under the barriers to get a closer look at an all-new prototype road car – the Model A Duesenberg. The car pioneered the straight-eight engine, which becomes the preferred engine configuration of the decade. It also introduced four-wheel brakes with hydraulic actuation, the most important chassis and safety improvement for years to come, four years ahead of Chrysler. This proved to be a pivotal visit for Virgil. He was an avid collector of automobilia and ephemera, especially car brochures. Following the show, he frequently wrote to the Duesenberg factory in Indianapolis requesting information on its car. So enthusiastic were his letters to the company that Harold Ames, the President of Duesenberg, personally replied to Virgil with an offer to drive a Model A from the Chicago showroom to the Exner home so that Virgil could take a ride. Oddly, he never replied to the letter and ceased his communications with the company, but the boy's love of cars, and 'Duesys' in particular, was cemented.

From September 1921, Virgil studied at the newly rebuilt Buchanan High School, 401 West Chicago Street, where he excelled in music, science, literacy (he joined the school literary society in his final year), sport,

Buchanan High School in Michigan was rebuilt in 1922 and was the place that gave the young Virgil Exner his first opportunity to display his artistic talent, sometimes to the annoyance of his teachers. (Buchanan High School)

Opposite: 1924. The yearbooks at Buchanan High School gave Virgil his first opportunity to publish his art work. From 1924 through to 1926, he illustrated the chapter headings and did some of the sponsorship adverts. I(Buchanan High School)

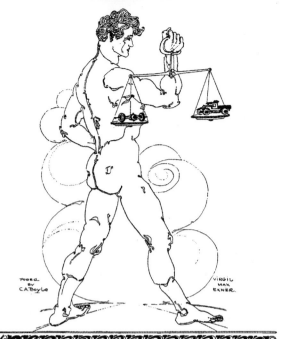

Athletics

The Smart Set of '26

	GIRL	BOY
Best Liked	Helen Lyon	Jerry Mann
Best Looking	Eva Ellis	Harvey Reed
Best All-Round	Beth Batchelor	Bernard Brown
Best Natured	Agnes Koenigshof	Bob Rinker
Cleverest	Josphine Gross	Arthur Allen
Worst Giggler	Viola Fitch	Milton Mitchell
Hottest Tempered	Ione Riley	Frank Chain
Night Hawks	Hildred Hanover	Bob Rinker
Most Motherly & Fatherly	Beth Batchelor	Walter Scott
Most Bashful	Virginia Hess	Lee Lister
Biggest Flirt	Viola Fitch	Clarence Wangerin
Worst Primper	Esther Elber	Virgil Exner
Teacher's Pet	Grace Letcher	Bob Hall
Most Accommodating	Beth Batchelor	Walter Scott
Most Athletic	Lorraine Haas	Herbert Batchelor
Best Cook	Agnes Koenigshof	Vine Cook
Most Ambitious	Clarabel Myers	Floyd Fedore
Most Likely to Succeed	Josephine Gross	Jerry Mann
Best Student	Grace Letcher	Bernard Brown
Class Angel	Virginia Hess	Donald Rhoades
Worst Gum Chewer	Arlene Stevens	Virgil Exner
Champion Bluffer	Hildred Hanover	Gerrett Wisner
Class Clown	Viola Fitch	Floyd Bailey
Biggest Booster	Grace Letcher	Walter Scott
Slangiest Person	Hildred Hanover	DeLoss Proceus
Biggest Eater	Ione Riley	Arthur Allen
Greatest Talker	Josephine Gross	Floyd Bailey
Most Graceful	Ione Riley	Babe Mills
Best Dancer	Helen Lyon	Donald White
Most Musical	Esther Elber	Chester Wooley
Biggest Baby	Esther Eilber	Donald White
Best Duck Hunter		Jerry Mann

Nameless, Senseless, Plotless Verse

Elizabeth Kiehn

When from school we are dismissed,
A diploma in our fist,
We'll look back with gladsome mood
Thinking that we turned out—good.

If ourselves we could but see,
We'd begin to think that we
Weren't so bright as first we thought.
See that we turned out as *Naught*.

and of course, art. Latin was his strongest subject, with commercial law, typewriting and chemistry being his weakest. He was tall, slim, athletic, and devilishly handsome. Later in life colleagues would later describe Virgil's appearance as 'well-groomed', 'well-dressed', 'clothed in fine Italian suits', and his enthusiasm for neat presentation started in high school, becoming so much a signature, even by the standards of the sophisticated and smart 1920s set, that fellow classmates light-heartedly ribbed Virgil within the pages of the annual yearbooks. In the 1924 issue, friends noted on the 'Just Imagine' page: "'Virg' Exner – With his hair mussed up." The following year they wrote: "The world will come to an end when ... Virgil Exner runs out of Hair-Groom." Due to his constant preening, in his senior year he was awarded the honour of 'Worst primper' along with the ignominious title of 'Worst gum chewer'.

So it was at Buchanan High that he started to draw and even design his own automobile bodies including Duesenberg designs and a Kissel Roadster. Further encouraged by both his art teacher, Miss Minshall, who also happened to board at the Exner's home, and his mother, Iva, Virgil's talent blossomed. Along with another good friend, Lee Lister, 'Virg' soon became the high school cartoonist and yearbook artist as well as becoming the Class Secretary in his final year. The yearbooks, dubbed 'The Pines' were important to Virgil, giving him his earliest opportunity to publish artwork. Not only did he draw the chapter headers, where his wry sense of humor came to the fore, he also drew some of the adverts for local companies that sponsored the printing of the yearbooks. The most noteworthy was the one for Clarke Axles, which featured a Grecian god-like figure holding what appears to be a Studebaker truck. A remarkable choice of subject considering what the future held for the young artist. Even

Jerry Mann

Donald Rhoades

Virginia Hess

Viola Fitch

Arthur Allen

Lyle Wynn

Clarabelle Meyers

Grace Letcher

Virgil Exner

DeLos Proseus

at the tender age of 16, Virgil knew exactly where his future lay, so did his friends. In a prophetic statement, his senior yearbook saw one of his class mates write of his qualities:

*With such a pencil, such a pen
Your name will be with famous men.*

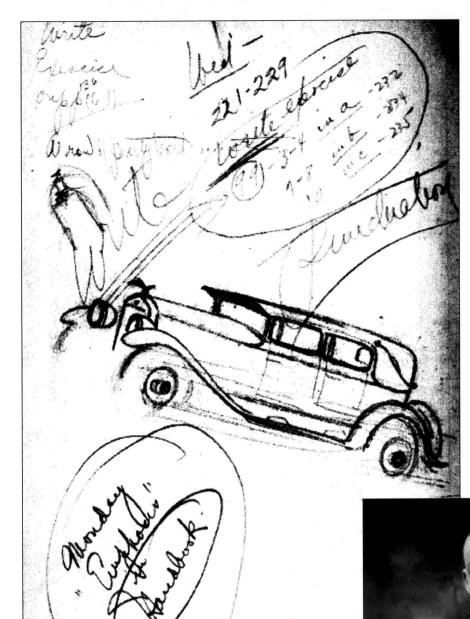

as ironic that Virgil's first girlfriend was also named after a car: Mercedes Capen from nearby Niles, Michigan.

George still supported Virgil's interest in automobiles and, in May 1923, he took his son to see their first Indianapolis 500 race. The thrill of watching his beloved Duesenberg and Miller-powered race cars thundering around the Brickyard was a dream come true. As an added bonus for the young boy, the elegant Duesenberg Model A paced this 11th Indy 500, driven by Fred Duesenberg. The trip was not without incident, a race car lost control and ploughed into the spectators, killing one spectator, narrowly missing Virgil, and hitting George, breaking his leg. George vowed never to go back to the Brickyard but Virgil had caught the racing bug and would return to Indianapolis on many occasions.

Although not Catholic (nor a follower of any religion), on graduating from Buchanan High on 11th June

Not all of his teachers appreciated his earliest work as he constantly sketched vehicles in the margins of his workbooks whilst sitting in class. Although very shy, by his early teens, this handsome, smartly-dressed young man had discovered the fairer sex, and it could be seen

1926. This graduation photo shows an intelligent young man ready to start university at Notre Dame.

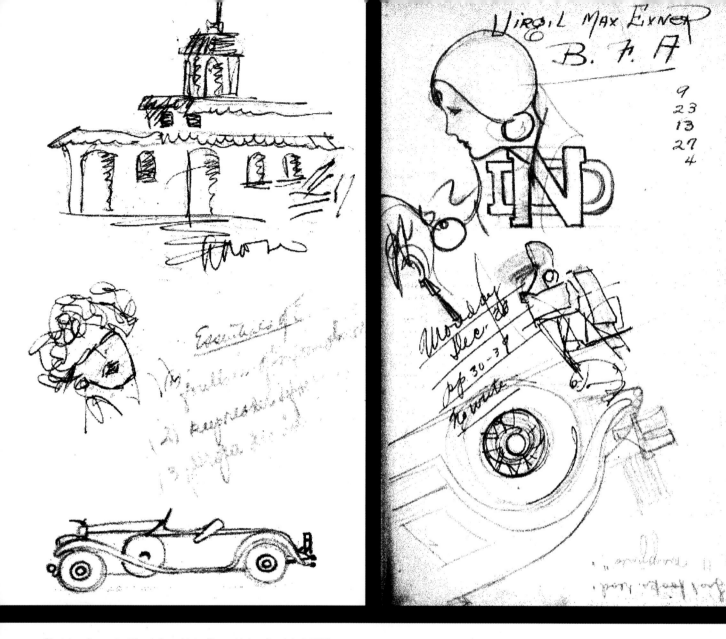

Sketches from a text book from Notre Dame University, dated 1926.

1926, age 16, and still with just elementary artistic training, this tall (5ft 11in), quietly spoken young man, managed to enrol as a day student at the nearby College of Arts and Letters at the all-male Catholic University of Notre Dame. He started there on 13th September 1926.

Iva had taught Virgil and George how to drive in the family's first car, a Willy's Overland Whippet, which enabled Virgil to commute to university in his first car, a 1921 Model T Ford. Even this most mundane of cars received the Exner touch; Virgil added a Duesenberg emblem, a LeBaron nameplate and gold pinstriping to the belt-line and door, for a fancier hot rod look. The quiet, dusty roads of Buchanan were often disturbed as his snorting, shivering, bone-shaker 'Tin Lizzie' raced through the town, waking and upsetting neighbors. When not behind the wheel of his car, he was a quiet, mild mannered, but sometimes precocious child, but at the wheel of an automobile he became a speed demon. School friends remember that every time he managed to race past a heavier and more powerful car, he would pull over and carve another notch in his steering wheel, much as gun-fighters used to do in the Wild West. They also say that it was around this time that he started to call himself 'Ex' as he thought 'Virgil' sounded too feminine.

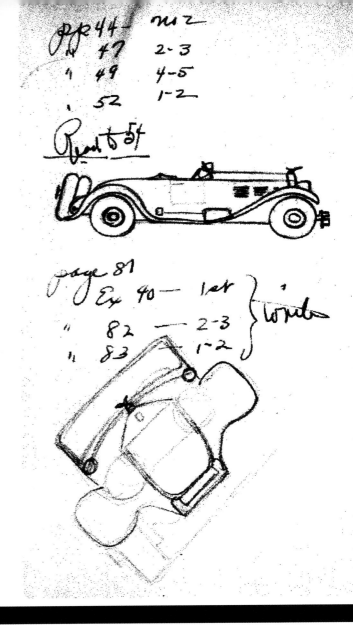

Virgil spent the next two years studying as a day student at Notre Dame majoring in art, where he gained very high marks, also gaining the habit of smoking, too, which would adversely affect his health later in life. George and Iva, with Virgil working occasional jobs as a signwriter, primarily paid for his fees. Virgil studied French but struggled with the language. Consistent high marks were gained in English, history and art. In the second semester of his first year, he had his first opportunity to study commercial art along with more traditional forms. It must have been somewhat of a relief when in his second term, French was replaced with elementary Latin, where he excelled again. The money to cover his tuition fees started to dwindle as costs increased but it was advice from the head of the art department, Professor Ernest Thompson that helped Virgil make his decision to leave. Virgil had been giving most of his attention to fine art and painting skills, along with the classes in basic design and advertising art. Virgil was told that Notre Dame could not teach him much more than he already knew and if he wanted a career in advertising art then he should look for employment on the fringes of that business. So, in 1928, Virgil left university without graduating, two years into his four year course, and decided to hunt down a job, but where to look?

South Bend, Indiana, lies just 12 miles from Buchanan and, as well as being home to the University of Notre Dame, was one of the main employment areas in that part of the country, so it was only natural for Virgil to look for work there. He was advised to visit Advertising Artists, Inc, which was an advertising studio branch of the then well-established Meinzinger Studios of Detroit and Chicago. Run by Frank C Foote from Detroit and Ed Clarke in South Bend, this company held many important accounts, including Clarke Equipment, Conn Instruments, Berghoff Brewery, and, most importantly, the Studebaker account, a company that had had its headquarters in South Bend since 1852.

Ed Clarke's newly appointed young secretary, Mildred Marie Eshleman, had shown Exner into the office for his interview. A recent graduate from South Bend's Business College, she seemed quite pleased when Ed agreed to

In 1929, with regular money coming in, Ex traded in his old Model T hot rod for a newer Ford Model A roadster. With its tan body, black fenders and cerise wheels, it was a sharp-looking car.

take the attractive young man on as an errand boy. She filled out the required paperwork giving Virgil Max Exner his first real job. As the ambitious new recruit ran errands delivering artwork and prints to various local clients, he got the opportunity to get to know the illustrators at Advertising Artists, design engineers at Studebaker, and Mildred, much better.

In October 1929, the stock markets crashed and the worst depression to hit America arrived. The Exner family found itself in a relatively strong position, with George and Virgil both employed. Work, for those that had it, did not reduce. In an effort to keep their heads above water, most

Mildred Marie Eshleman worked in administration at Advertising Artists, Inc and was the person that handled the paperwork giving Virgil Exner his first job.

Ex started at Advertising Artists, Inc as an office gopher and courier, but soon began working on the boards. This brochure for local instrument maker Conn was one of Exner's first major jobs.

Virgil soon became one of the main illustrators for the prestigious Studebaker account. These two drawings, taken from the 1931 brochure, show a yellow President Four-Season convertible roadster and an elegant St Regis Brougham two-door sedan.

companies tried to increase production wherever possible. The hours were long and the pay was low but it was a job, and one that Virgil enjoyed, being close to artists, soaking up the abundance of knowledge around him. Virgil occasionally showed Ed Clarke some of the work that he had being doing at home. With the questions that he asked and the interest that he showed, it wasn't too

long before the office gofer was given a chance to show what he could do.

Under the direction of Frank Foote and Ed Clarke, Virgil was offered the chance to work on the 'boards', initially doing some backgrounds for Studebaker car illustrations. For the most part these early works

On 7th March 1931, Virgil married Mildred. This is thought to be the only surviving photo of that day.

1931. The young couple just after their wedding in South Bend, Indiana.

This picture, taken outside the Exner family home in South Bend in the summer of 1933, shows the proud father with his son, Virgil Jr.

were done as transparent watercolors and were well-received. Over the next two years, Virgil went from doing backgrounds to illustrating Studebaker trucks and cars. He spent six years at Advertising Artists, Inc, learning and honing his design, drafting and artistic skills.

In 1929, with regular money coming in, Ex traded in his old Model T hot rod for a newer Ford Model A Roadster. With its tan body, black fenders and cerise wheels, it was a sharp looking car. This same year Virgil also finally bucked up the courage to ask Mildred out on a date, which she promptly accepted. To Virgil's surprise, it soon became apparent that Mildred shared his love of fast cars, so many of their dates were spent at local dirt track races in the Michigan area.

Whilst working on various accounts including Studebaker, Conn Instruments, McCray Refrigerators, etc., Virgil was working on his own ideas. At this time, there was no recognized profession of automobile design, or even industrial design, except where coachbuilders had an 'in-house' designer, but Virgil kept at it, working on advanced designs, mainly inspired from the race cars he admired. Even at this early point in his career, he had a very clear idea of what contemporary automobiles should look like and how they would look in the future. Vehicles

This snapshot was taken in 1932 at a lake near Buchanan. As well as showing his athletic physique, the picture also captures the look of rebelliousness that ran through Exner which would manifest itself later in his career.

The front cover of the Studebaker brochure for 1932, drawn by Exner.

from European manufacturers inspired Ex to adopt a clean, sharp line to his drawings.

In late 1930 he proposed to Mildred and they married on 7th March the following year in a small church ceremony in Buchanan. Until that time, Mildred had been boarding with a family called the Schaefers, where she had initially been a housekeeper and live-in babysitter while she was studying. Virgil had been commuting daily from Buchanan to South Bend but, upon marriage,

they rented an apartment in an older part of town. Despite suffering the hardships of the Depression, the young professional couple were happy, the young dreamer and his astute, strong-willed wife, surviving on a combined wage of just $11.44 a week. Even at this early stage in their relationship, Mildred put her foot down and decreed that Exner was not allowed to smoke in the house, which he duly accepted. Within sixteen months Mildred fell pregnant, and on 17th April 1933, she gave birth to a boy, who they named Virgil Max Exner Jr.

By now, Virgil was designing the complete Studebaker brochure, and outsiders were noticing his work. A local newspaper wanted to do an article on the future of the

By 1933, Exner was creating the entire brochure for Studebaker. This yellow sedan is just one of the beautiful illustrations he crafted.

HARTER STEEL POSTURE CHAIRS

BAD SEATING
Cripples Health, Morale and Production
★

FOR BETTER HEALTH · GREATER COMFORT · IMPROVED WORK

Front cover of Posture Chairs brochure from 1935.

MODERN FOOD MERCHANDISING
is built around More and Better
DISPLAY

In the design and construction of this new case McCray has brought to bear an experience of 44 years in meeting every refrigeration need in the food store. A glance at the case instantly reveals a new note of attention-compelling beauty. The simplicity and correctness of its lines and the absence of metal strips and screws enhance the fine appearance of the gleaming porcelain exterior with its moulded panels, black base and trim.

The correctly sloped front . . . undivided plate glass across the entire case . . . . and the improved exterior lighting system are all features which increase the visibility and enhance the sales value of food displayed in this case.

The rear of the new McCray case is of oak, finished silver-gray. Sliding doors of wood, finished black . . . with two thicknesses of double strength glass . . . glide smoothly on black porcelain runways. Wrapping counter 8¼″ wide extends across entire back. Scale stand, in center, accommodating any standard size scale is 18″ x 20″ and 30½″ from floor. This new model is exceptionally easy to work out of since any part of the display compartment is readily reached.

McCRAY REFRIGERATOR SALES CORP.
108 McCRAY COURT
Kendallville, Indiana

Salesrooms in All Principal Cities

See Telephone Directory

REFRIGERATORS BY *McCray*

Model

REAR OF MODEL 108

				Sq. Ft.	Cu. Ft.		
Model	Length	Depth	Height	Single Shelf	Capacity	Shipping Weight	Code Word
88	8′	2′10″	4′2″	17.89	20.25	1350	Davenport
108	10′	2′10″	4′2″	22.36	25.6	1550	Deluxe
128	12′	2′10″	4′2″	27.	30.9	1550	Dublin
Compartment	Model	Width	Depth	Height	Door Opening		
Cooling Chamber	88	9½″	28½″	8½″	4 doors, 33″ x 13½″		
Cooling Chamber	108	11½″	28½″	8½″	4 doors, 24″ x 13½″		
Cooling Chamber	128	13½″	29½″	8½″	4 doors, 24″ x 13½″		

These models are also available with refrigerated base.
For further description see back page of this folder.

108

Illustrating or laying out brochures for many industrial appliances was everyday work for Exner. This is the center spread for McCray refrigerators from 1934.

Studebaker presents for 1934 ... A change in style for the illustrations of that year's brochure.

automobile, and Exner was asked to supply the artwork and his thoughts on design progression. This gave Exner some much-needed publicity but it was visits from Advertising Artists top management that finally gave him the break he needed. Ed Meinsinger, one of the principals of Advertising Artists, took a keen interest in what was happening in the South Bend studio. On his many visits he would often discuss some of the futuristic designs that were pinned around Exner's drafting cubicle. Meinsinger knew Harley Earl, the head of General Motors Art and Color Department, and he also knew that Earl was looking for fresh talent. Meinsinger suggested to Virgil that he get a portfolio of his work together while he organized a meeting with Earl.

Late in 1933, Virgil made the trip to Detroit to talk with Harley Earl and Howard O'Leary, Earl's second-in-command and administration chief. He was told that it was Earl's wish to increase the Art and Color Section

from fifty staff to over two hundred. This ambitious plan would utilise the expanding pool of artists, engineers and designers that were being laid off from other companies as luxury custom coachbuilders closed their doors. It was Earl's intention to take the cream of this crop to add to his already talented team. Exner was offered a job the same day, which he accepted immediately.

The young family moved to 15736 Ohio Street, a top floor apartment in the New Center area of Detroit very early in 1934 so that Exner could take up his position within Earl's Art and Color Section, located on the third floor of the General Motors Building. He treated himself to a new car, yet another Ford, this time it was a dark green coupe with custom light green pinstriping. Because of its excellent handling qualities, this became one of Exner's favorite cars.

Initially, he worked under Franklin (Frank) Q Hershey, the head of the Pontiac studio. With an embryonic

Just two years on and the family had moved to 15736 Ohio Street, a top floor apartment in the New Center area of Detroit.

General Motor's Art and Color Section was a basic workhouse for designers. Long hours and poor conditions were accepted as part of the lifestyle.

philosophy of style developing, the designers at General Motors enjoyed a great deal of flexibility, resulting in exciting and diverse designs. Accomplished designers like Gordon Buehrig, Frank Hershey, Bill Mitchell, Clare MacKichan, Paul Meyer and Ned Nickles, amongst others, all spent time in the new Art and Color Section and were joined by the likes of Clare Hodgeman, Paul Zimmerman and Carl Reynolds, as well as Exner. This mix of fresh young blood and experienced designers worked very well. Highlights at this time for Exner were being involved with the 1936 Buick (taking over from Paul Meyer) and having some input in the 1935/36 Pontiac production models; he is credited with designing the Silver Streak trim – bright metal strips that ran from the cowl, forward along the hood and down the front of the radiator. Although the Pontiacs shared bodies with Chevrolet, the Silver Streaks alone made the newly streamlined Pontiacs instantly recognizable, with the new trim becoming a Pontiac hallmark for the next twenty years. In 1973, writer Richard M Langworth asked Exner if he had been responsible for them, and knowing that he did not like garish ornamentation on his cars, was he sorry he did

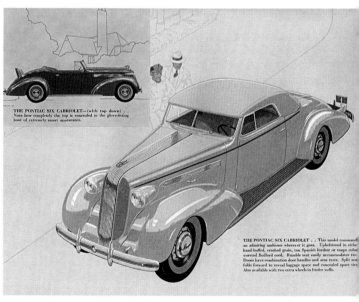

Exner is credited with creating the Silver Streak brightwork that adorned Pontiac hoods for more than two decades, although some historians would argue that it was Frank Hershey who designed the flamboyant waterfall style, seen here on a 1936 Cabriolet.

it. Ex replied with humor, "Yes to both questions. It was all I could do when I first took over. I thought we needed something to unify the round-top grille with the rest of the car. It worked for a while. Of course, Pontiac got stuck on it, and it lasted far too long." In his book, *Pontiac, the complete history*, Thomas E Bonsall quotes Frank Hershey as the creator of the Silver Streaks. Hershey said that the design first appeared on a clay model used in one of Earl's competitions as early as 1933, and was inspired by the finned oil canister from a Napier race car, a full twelve months before Exner started working for GM. Undoubtedly, Exner did modify the design for the 1937 and '38 models.

To spur on his team to even greater heights, and to increase competitiveness between the divisional studios of Pontiac, Chevrolet, Buick, Oldsmobile and Cadillac, Harley Earl held an annual design competition within his section. Each designer that held any relatively major responsibility was given the task of coming up with a design and clay model for the contest. Earl knew that with an ever-increasing amount of staff, there had to be more structure to the department, with clear echelons of superiority. Unbeknownst to the contestants, the competition held in the fall of 1934 would decide the new heads of the various divisional design studios. Up against senior and other junior designers, Exner was one of the winners, along with Clare Hodgeman and Paul Zimmerman. In early 1935, just a few months after the competition, Frank Hershey took control of the Cadillac studio and then Opel, and Exner found himself the new head of the Pontiac Studio, the youngest person ever to hold that position at the tender age of twenty-six.

Both Virgil and Mildred enjoyed their time in Detroit, mixing with a group of young artistic individuals living in the immediate vicinity of the New Center area. Clare Hodgeman, now head of Oldsmobile, and his twin sister Clarise, Carl Reynolds, and Paul Zimmerman (Chief Stylist at Chevrolet, and clay modeler George Martin were amongst this tight-knit band. Whilst socializing, talk would inevitably turn to the future of auto design. The group would buy as many European car magazines as they could find, and were particularly inspired by the smooth clean lines of race cars of the time, especially Mercedes, Auto Union, Alfa Romeo, and Maserati. Virgil and Mildred were regular visitors to the ½ mile dirt track speedway at East 8 Mile Road, and any kind of car race was enough to draw them to a venue. One of Virgil Jr's first memories is of the regular visits to that speedway. Ex would always be buying his son toy cars and, of course, draw pictures for him. Christmas 1936 saw the arrival of Junior's first kiddie-car, which Ex customized with pinstriping and decals, adding his own favorite number 5 to the side. With the younger Exner's arrival, Mildred called her husband Virg and Junior was called Virgil.

The young group of friends found themselves at the cutting edge of, and heading, an industrial design revolution. GM vehicles were setting the style of the times with all-steel streamlined cars that featured rakish radiator grilles, smooth fenders and V-shaped windscreens. This move away from the 'classic' horseless carriage and squared-off vehicles of the teens and twenties was a quantum leap for automobiles. Up to the mid-thirties, styling was predominantly the responsibility of the engine and body engineers, with yearly restyling only amounting to different radiator grilles and mild ornamentation. With engineers calling the shots, almost all North American automobiles looked very similar indeed, and, although for the most part they were reliable and in some cases even over-engineered, style was not their priority. Style, however, was becoming more important to the buying public. Harley Earl's Art and Color Section worked in partnership with engineers to produce a car that looked as good as it performed, and as divisional identities within General Motors became more important, so did the emphasis on styling. A philosophy was being born that would influence car design forever.

Earl wanted smooth, flowing lines, with exterior parts 'built in' to the design, blending with the whole. The rear bumper would match the front, the interior handles and winders were sculpted to match the exterior handles, and rear light bezels would complement the front. Every piece of ornamentation would look like it was designed to go with the basic body as well as every other detail. A vehicle became a complete piece, instead of many mismatched parts bolted together. Innovations in mass-produced steel bodies, glass, plastic technology and even fabrics, helped this continuity of design.

GM's A&C section also pioneered techniques to help the designer, most notably advances in clay modeling, which had begun in Europe but was embraced and developed mainly by Harley Earl around 1914. The specially produced clay was heated in large ovens to make it malleable. By using an oil-based compound instead of the traditional water-based clay, plaster or wood, stylists and modelers gained much-needed freedom to see their work in three-dimensions and to change details where necessary. Within the design process, this was the first time that the image was given physical form. Moving away from full-sized wooden mock-ups where clay was only used as a filling material, to a complete clay surface covering a rough wooden mannequin, allowed designers and bosses to gain a truer sense of the design's size, proportions and character, relatively quickly and at less cost. The finished model was a product of refined craftsmanship, one so detailed that it was difficult to distinguish from a real car. Using the mannequin underneath instead of solid clay also helped to keep the weight down so that they could be moved

The 1938 Pontiac was the first complete car that Ex had control over styling, and he was happy with the outcome, if not the ride. He owned a four-door sedan, but complained that the drive was lousy compared to his Studebaker. Although the crowds are flocking around the cars in this photo, taken in a Pontiac dealership, the cars were not as successful as GM had hoped.

around, but, even so, the models still weighed more than three times what a real car would. It wasn't all plain sailing, however. There was no air conditioning in the clay modeling studio, hot or cold, and when the temperature dropped significantly, the clay would crack, and the front end would fall off the models. These scale models were lined up in one long room but the designers worked in another room. They were, of course, allowed to look at the models, but they could not work alongside them, which greatly hindered their progress.

Virgil was at the forefront of this cutting edge design concept and embraced it wholeheartedly. His earliest major work at GM was the Pontiac for 1937 and its face-lift for 1938. This was the first complete car that Virgil had responsibility for, and, surprisingly perhaps, one he wasn't very happy with. All new in 1937, the longer, trimmer

Deluxe Sixes and Eights featured rounder bodies and a sportier, wider nose. Ex had nimbly lowered the belt-line and added gentle creases to the fenders, offering the illusion of lowness. The following year he added a larger, handsome Cord-like grille. Virgil Jr recalls that his father arrived home one day early in 1938 at the wheel of his brand new maroon 4-door Pontiac. His father's pride, as was the family's, was justifiably immense but Exner Senior thought that the car was a lousy vehicle mechanically. He thought that the handling characteristics and heating system of his '34 Ford were better than the new Pontiac.

Financially, the vehicles were not as successful as GM hoped. Going into a major recession in that year,

Opposite: The automotive industry got stylists to patent their own designs and then paid them $1 to use that design. This patent for a bumper was filed on 2nd February 1938 and was the first of many to be submitted by Ex.

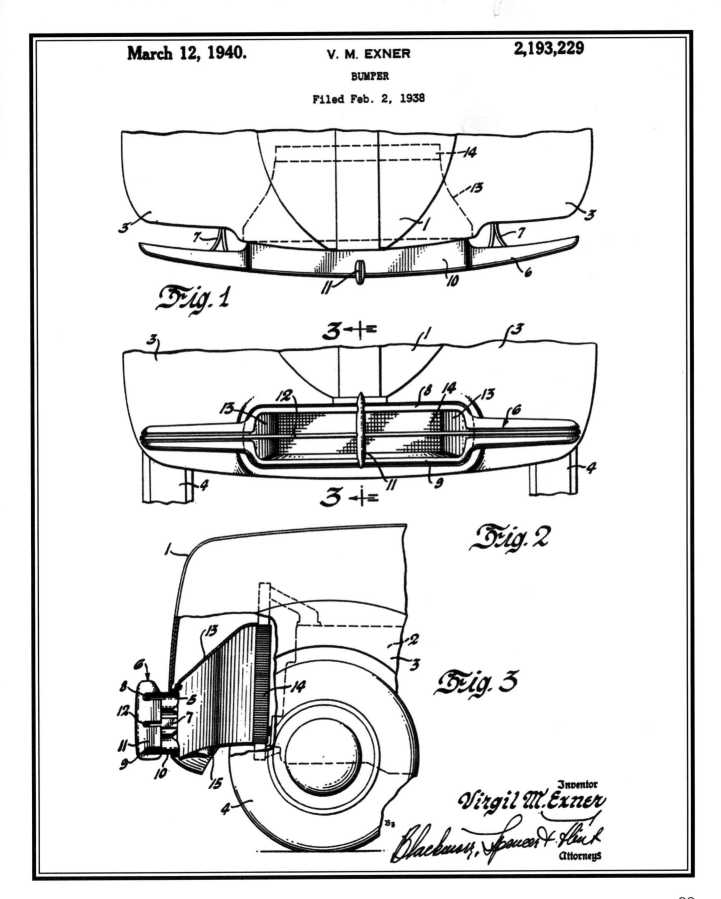

Fig. 1

Fig. 2

Fig. 3

Inventor
Virgil M. Exner

Blackmur, Spencer & Flint
Attorneys

23

This sketch, done by Ex in October 1937, shows the patented air intake grille fitted to a car. Interesting to note that this suggestion for a 1939 Pontiac has no Silver Streak brightwork.

sales plummeted by nearly 140,000 units on the previous year's production, causing Pontiac to drop behind Dodge in the manufacturers league. During this period, Virgil also helped out on other projects and even patented some of the designs, most notably the headlights for the 1939 Buick and an integrated bumper and grille. This latter design utilized the bumper as an air intake, taking air through a large conduit from the bumper directly to the radiator. GM used this jet-like grille design successfully and extensively, long after Exner's departure, on its late 1940s and early '50s vehicles. The Exners managed to get to Miami, Florida for a winter vacation, but they were the lucky ones. Working through the recession of 1938 and into 1939, the designers toiled long hours for an unimpressive wage, sometimes sacrificing their annual vacations to get urgent jobs finished. It was not unknown for Earl to make his staff work on Christmas Day. It was into this harsh working climate that industrial designer Raymond Loewy entered Exner's life.

Happy families in Miami Beach 1939. The Exners loved to vacation, and Florida remained one of their favorite destinations.

3 DANGEROUS CURVES AHEAD

Raymond Loewy had worked his way up from being a fashion illustrator to arguably the world's first industrial design guru. Loewy launched his career in industrial design in 1929 when Sigmund Gestetner, a British manufacturer of duplicating machines, commissioned him to improve the appearance of a mimeograph machine. In just three days, the 28-year-old Loewy designed the shell that was to sheath Gestetner duplicators for the next 40 years. In the process, he helped launch a profession that has changed the look of the modern world. Quite simply, Loewy streamlined everything he could, from company logos like Shell, Exxon and Greyhound to locomotives, refrigerators, spacecraft and cola bottles. His concept of 'beauty through function and simplification' was the beginning of industrial design as a legitimate profession. By 1938, Raymond Loewy was almost a household name, with his company handling design work for many large American companies, amongst whom were International Truck, Pennsylvania Railroad, Coca-Cola and Studebaker.

Studebaker had gone through a rough patch in the early thirties, with falling sales, a failed merger, and the resignation and subsequent suicide of its long time President, Albert Russell Erskine. By 1937, sales had improved under the leadership of Studebaker Vice Presidents for Production and Sales, Harold S Vance and Paul G Hoffman. They felt that without an in-house design department of their own, the success might be short-lived. Hoffman had seen the work that Loewy had done on the 1932-34 Hupmobile and offered him a contract to establish a design department at Studebaker headquarters in South Bend and come up with a fresh design for 1938. With the promise of the new automobile account under his belt, Raymond Loewy went on a talent search, and his first stop was General Motors. As much as they liked Harley Earl, with the chance of doubling their pay packets, as well as working for the famed R Loewy in his prestigious New York offices, such an offer was irresistible for some of his prized designers. First to go was Clare Hodgeman from Oldsmobile, and then Paul Zimmerman from Chevrolet, and finally Exner was lured away from Pontiac.

In 1938, Mildred, Virgil and Junior made the move to New York, where Loewy had his headquarters, renting a house in the Amityville area of Long Island. Virgil commuted the short distance into the city to Loewy's studio on 33rd and Broadway, joining his friends Clare Hodgeman and Paul Zimmerman, who were already working on designs for 'interurban' railway passenger carriages and some architectural contracts. Ex worked on coach design for the Pennsylvania Railroad, but Loewy knew that Exner hailed from South Bend and already had connections with Studebaker, so it was a logical choice to earmark him for the position of servicing the Studebaker account, along with overseeing the International Truck contract.

Ex joined Loewy in 1938 and the family moved to the Amityville area of Long Island, New York. Father and son shared a common love of all things wheeled. This picture was taken outside their apartment in 1939.

First port of call was to Fort Wayne to work on the International Truck line for 1939, which was quickly completed, and then Exner turned his attention to Studebaker. Although Paul Hoffman had requested an in-house design team to be situated at Studebaker's facilities in Indiana, Loewy initially set them to work in his own New York offices, with Exner having to commute to Studebaker's South Bend plant, staying for a week at a time, every three weeks. He trained to Indiana and stayed with his parents during the week then took the 'midnight flyer' train back to New York for the weekend. During holidays, it was quite common for him to be accompanied by Virgil Jr on these trips. Exner endured this grueling schedule until 1941 when he finally moved his family back to South Bend.

Exner's first task at Studebaker was to tidy-up the design for its all-new 1939 model, the Champion. The Champion was a shorter vehicle than its Commander or President stablemates, but shared a common design

Mildred proudly holds her second son, Brian Leigh, just weeks after his birth.

Virgil Sr with his two sons, Virgil Jr and Brian, July 1940.

theme that had come from Clare Hodgeman of the Loewy studio in the previous year. A prominent prow-type hood and grille accentuated the smoothness of the overhaul design. The pod headlamps from 1938 were replaced with lights integrated into the fenders and a more delicate butterfly-like grille featuring horizontal steel strips that gave a handsome finish. The sleeker 1938 and '39 models were very well-received, and the troubled Studebaker Company saw its sales double by 1939, due in no small part to the Champion, which even after its mid-season release still managed a staggering 34,000 sales. Roy Cole, the chief Studebaker engineer, along with Eugene Hardig, was behind the cleverly engineered Champion. Less powerful

than its competitors, but also lighter by nearly 600lb to its nearest rival, the Champion could achieve nearly 80mph from its 164.3in³ L-head six and could still boast about its robust build quality. In July 1939, two stock Champion 2-door sedans circled the Indianapolis racetrack for 15,000 miles with an average speed of 62mph, while achieving an average of 20mpg. This amazing publicity stunt swayed the Indy officials to select Studebaker as the official pace car for the following year's prestigious 500-mile race. Oddly, Studebaker chose to send a 1940 Champion 2-door coupe to pace the race instead of the more luxurious Commander or President. This was the first time that a closed car had paced the event. Ex gladly attended the

Although not blood relatives, Virgil and his father, George, appear strikingly similar in looks and build. This photo was taken in 1940 on a family picnic.

and suddenly swooped into Long Island and New England. In an area unused to such extreme weather conditions, nobody was prepared for the ensuing chaos. The result was death and destruction, with more than 500 lives lost, 57,034 homes destroyed or damaged, and a property loss that extended into hundreds of millions of dollars. For the Exner family it was a terrifying experience. Virgil senior was unable to cross from Manhattan to Long Island to get back to his family, who were confined to their home in Amityville. Virgil Jr then aged just five, recalls how terrifying it was. "We were home alone; Father was stuck in the city and couldn't get back right away as the commuter trains were out. We had no electricity, the basement was completely flooded, the roof was taking in water, and trees were being ripped out of the ground. Mother and I were scared to death, we huddled together in a small upstairs closet".

Exner made it home the next day and was relieved to find minimal damage to their home. They were lucky indeed.

Remaining on Long Island, in the early summer of 1939 the Exner family moved into 12 Plymouth Road, Port Washington, a select and prosperous new subdivision called New Salem. This two-storey all-brick house was designed and planned by the Exners including picking the exact plot, design, flooring and landscaping. Young Virgil Jr loved the new house and the neighbours; movie and Broadway star June Havoc, the younger sister of Gypsy Rose Lee, lived directly behind the Exners' home with her daughter April. They became great playmates. Ex and Mildred settled quickly into their 'dream home' and while Ex continued his commuting from New York to South Bend, Mildred created a beautiful home. By the September of 1939 she had become pregnant and on the 2nd June 1940, their second son, Brian Leigh was born.

The 1941 Studebakers received an all-new look for 1941 across the entire range that featured a sharper front end with a lower, wider grille. Although the Commander and low-volume President both saw increases in sales, again it was the Champion models that became a runaway success; with sales reaching almost 85,000 it became the highest selling line in the company's history. Virgil Exner was very pleased with the outcome and became a big fan of these cars, finally owning a series of them starting from 1939 with a Champion, then a Commander, up to a 1941 President, which he kept until 1947. The President was one of his all-time favorites and he came up with a special paint scheme of tulip crème with a dark green roof and thick dark green side stripe. So striking was this custom paint job, it later became a production option.

Although the team at Studebaker was extremely happy with Exner's work, they were still putting pressure

race, along with other Studebaker officials, to watch his design speed around the Brickyard. Exner worked directly with Cole whilst in South Bend, the stylist and engineer complimenting each other's work to find a shared direction with the design and cultivating a close friendship.

Exner still spent a lot of time at the New York office, and it was during one of these 'at home' periods that disaster struck. On the afternoon of 21st September 1938, he was at his drawing board when the Long Island Express rolled into town. The class 3 hurricane had roared its way up from the West Indies, at first threatening to cross Florida, but then turned north past Cape Hatteras

Studebaker 1941

Bend. Bob continues, "The first thing I had to do was to see a fellow by the name of Perry Sullivan, who was head of the body engineering division. They had a building on Sample Street, and it was divided. The chassis division was on one side, and there was a court in the middle, and the body division was on the other side, although there were walkways in between. Perry Sullivan interviewed me, and I showed him my things, and then he called Ex in. Ex came forward, and I met Ex for the first time. Perry said, 'Excuse me,' and he left me with Virg. Virgil looked at my stuff, and he said, 'Well, how would you like to work here?' I said, 'I would be very much interested.' He said, 'Do you think seventy-five bucks a week would do it for you?' At the time, I'd been raised from twenty-five bucks a week to forty dollars a week at Sears, and I said, "It's more money than I've ever heard of before." So I said, "Fine. When do you want me to start, now?" So after working two weeks notice at Sears, Bob joined Studebaker as Virgil's chief assistant. They were joined shortly after by expert clay modeler Frank Alhroth.

Across the automotive industry, these were busy times indeed. Work on the 1942, '43, '44 and '45 models had to be done, face-lift work on Studebaker's truck lines needed attention, and with the dark clouds of war looming on the horizon, government contracts were already coming in. A strong team of designers and modelers were hired by Exner, and many of them, such as John 'Jake' Aldrich, Bob Bingman, Tom Dingman and Frank Alhroth, went on to have very successful careers in their given fields of expertise. With a dedicated team of engineers allocated to the design house, work on outstanding projects progressed quickly. This almost autonomous team became known as the 'Loewy Gang' within the industry. Exner's charismatic and easygoing nature helped to cultivate an enjoyable and relaxed working environment, which in turn made for a productive outfit.

By the time America had entered World War II,

on Loewy to set up the design department in South Bend that they had initially requested. As well as the draining commuter life that Virgil endured, other problems arose. For the most part, Loewy gave his designers free reign, although they were not allowed to do any freelance work. Loewy, however, insisted on having the final say on designs, but with such infrequent visits by him to Studebaker, this caused delays in production. Finally, it was agreed that Exner and his family would move back permanently to South Bend so, in June of 1941, they rented out their home in Port Washington and returned to Indiana. What they found when they arrived was a housing shortage in the area, so the Exners rented a tiny pasteboard guest house on Donmoyer Street, part of the Paul G Hoffman estate, situated on the south side of South Bend. Virgil junior enrolled into the James Monroe Elementary School.

Once settled, Virgil senior could concentrate on building up an exclusive in-house Studebaker design team. In late 1940, Clare Hodgeman spoke with one of his old friends from his days at the Sears Roebuck design studio; his name was Robert (Bob) E Bourke. Clare told Bob that Ex was looking for a designer and that he should get some of his work together and bring it down to South

© 1945 The Studebaker Corporation

It's a jungle "Weasel" too!

STUDEBAKER'S amazing new Weasel personnel and cargo carrier is now in action in the Pacific islands—advancing, as it has been doing in Europe, over terrain that seems impossible for any mechanized military vehicle to negotiate.

The Weasel glides forward swiftly and stealthily in mud and swamp as well as on sand and snow—floats like a boat in lakes and rivers, as its powerful Studebaker Champion engine propels it from shore to shore.

This new "Champion" in invasion warfare not only transports men and supplies but also serves to carry wounded back to hospital areas. It's geared to clamber up seemingly impossible grades on its flexible, rubber-padded tracks.

Built by Studebaker, powered by the famous Studebaker Champion engine, the Weasel supplements such other Studebaker war production assignments as Wright Cyclone engines for the Boeing Flying Fortress and heavy-duty military trucks.

Awarded To All *Studebaker Plants*

Studebaker

PIONEER AND PACEMAKER
IN AUTOMOTIVE PROGRESS

Now building Wright Cyclone engines for the Boeing Flying Fortress — heavy-duty Studebaker military trucks—the Army's versatile personnel and cargo carrier, the Weasel.

YOUR WAR BONDS HELP KEEP THE FLYING FORTRESSES FLYING

Keep on buying War Bonds and keep the War Bonds you buy. They're the world's best investment. Every $3 you put up comes back to you worth $4.

Studebaker craftsmen again give "more than they promise"

The devastating bombing power and matchless fighting power of the Boeing Flying Fortress make comforting daily items in the war news.

Studebaker, America's oldest manufacturer of highway transportation, is privileged to collaborate with Wright, America's oldest producer of airplane engines, in providing flying power for this invincible dreadnaught of the skies. And Studebaker is also building much other war matériel, including tens of thousands of big, multiple-drive military trucks for the forces of the United Nations.

Today, as for generations past, Studebaker craftsmen make their watchword—*"give more than you promise."* Every Studebaker employee is justly proud of the achievements of his organization in the arming of our Nation and its Allies.

BUY U. S. WAR BONDS

War Trucks for the United Nations! Studebaker, famed for years for dependable transportation, has now become one of the largest producers of big, multiple-drive military trucks for the forces of the United Nations.

Studebaker BUILDS WRIGHT CYCLONE ENGINES FOR THE *Flying Fortress*

Studebaker was already heavily involved in design and production of military equipment. The 1942 models wore a wider, slightly heavier looking front end and utilized an all-new semi-automatic transmission called the 'Turbo-matic drive'. Production figures were high, with over 50,000 units built in the much-shortened model year. All of Studebaker's factories ceased civilian production in February 1942 and became part of America's mighty war machine. Along with the big US6 cargo truck, which was built in large numbers and many variations, the company's factories produced a large array of hardware including the Wright Cyclone aerial engine used on the B-17 Flying Fortress. In the design studio, many of the team left for military service. Exner was offered a commission in the Navy, but was persuaded that he could do more good

1942 DUKW Duck. The DUKW was built by General Motors and was based on its 2½ ton truck chassis. The hull was produced by boat designers, Sparkman & Stephens with help from Virgil Exner on the superstructure. The 'Duck', as it was affectionately known to the allied forces, could carry 5000lb of cargo or 25 fully-equipped troops. More than 21,000 were built through the war by GM, and 2000 were used in the Normandy landings of D-Day on 6th June 1944. The DUKW got its name from its military coding: D= Year of origin - 1942, U = Amphibian, K = All-wheel drive, W = Dual rear axle. (David Welch)

in his role as chief designer, so he stayed. He worked on many contracts but two that he was particularly pleased with were the amphibious DUKW (or 'Duck') cargo truck, built mainly by GMC, and the much smaller amphibious Weasel, both of which saw action in Europe and other theatres around the world.

The Duck was first introduced into service in 1943, serving first in Sicily, then on through the Italian and

1943 Weasel M-29. Along with the DUKW, this was Exner's most successful military design. The Weasel was produced between 1942 and 1945, with some 4476 T-24/M-29s being built, and more than 10,600 of the fully amphibious M-29C' before hostilities ended. The T-24/M-29 could carry a wide variety of cargo or personnel, enabling it to be used as command, radio, ambulance, signal-line laying, or light cargo vehicle. (Gary P Szechy)

north-west European campaigns and also in the Pacific, although the tracked LVT series was more common there and in Burma. It continued in military service for many years after the war, several finding their way into civilian agencies as emergency and rescue vehicles, while others have been used with varying degrees of modification as pleasure craft, and several preserved examples appear at vehicle rallies and as museum pieces. Two brightly painted yellow Ducks are a common sight on the crowded streets of London, England as tourist vehicles around Westminster and on the River Thames.

The story behind the Weasel is interesting. The Germans were producing heavy water in Norway, a vital component in the process of manufacturing atomic weapons. The archetypal English 'boffin' Geoffrey Pyke came up with the idea of a Commando raid on the factory, using the newly formed Commando Special Forces battalion. For any chance of success, they needed a special vehicle, one that could move quickly and easily through the winter snows of Norway. It needed to be air transportable and able to withstand being dropped by parachute. Intended specifically for quick assaults, it would also have to carry arms, explosives, and minimal re-supply stocks. This was a time-sensitive mission that required the engineering and building of an entirely new and innovative vehicle. The task of building the Weasel was undertaken by the Studebaker Company. Studebaker was given 180 days to produce a war-ready vehicle. By August 1942, less than 60 days after the commission was ordered, Exner and Roy Cole had come up with a workable design and were testing the prototype. Powered by a sturdy 6-170, 65hp straight-six Studebaker Champion engine, the Weasel was controlled, as most tracked vehicles are, by two tillers, one for each set of tracks (tracked vehicles with one engine are usually steered by braking one track or the other). As an added bonus, the Weasel prototype could float.

The first prototype M-29 'Weasel' carried the designation 'Cargo Carrier, Light T-24', the 'T' standing for 'test model'. The designation changed from T-24 to M-29 at serial number 1003. An impressive 4476 T-24/M-29s were produced from 1942 to 1945, and more than 10,600 M-29Cs were produced before hostilities ended. The T-24/M-29 could carry a wide variety of cargo or personnel, enabling it to be used as command, radio, ambulance, signal line laying, and light cargo vehicle. This tough little vehicle could carry up to four troops (including the driver) and proved most useful on difficult terrain (snow, swamps, sand, deep mud and lakes, etc). In 1943, Studebaker released the M-29C, a fully amphibious version that added watertight cells for buoyancy and twin rudders at the stern. Unfortunately, the Norwegian mission was cancelled and the Weasel was never used for its original intention,

although a different mission was successfully executed in February 1943 by Norwegian commandos, and portrayed in the Hollywood movie *The Heroes of Telemark*. It is thought that a Weasel was the first vehicle to land on Omaha Beach, on June 6th 1944. It proved very useful on winter terrain in the 1950s, when they were used in polar expeditions. It was used in vital Arctic and Antarctic operations, supporting explorers and scientists. As a testimony to their strength and durability, many are still in use today, in countries as far flung as Sweden, England and Canada, some sixty-plus years after they were built.

By the spring of 1942, the Exner family had moved to more comfortable accommodation when they rented a large farm house from Paul G Hoffman, situated on the southeast side of South Bend city limits at 1425 East Woodside Street. During that summer, Ex fulfilled a dream

Dude ranch photos. Since early childhood, Ex had felt passionate about the Old Wild West. In 1942, he and Mildred took the opportunity of living the life when they stayed at a dude range in Montana. The western hat accentuated Exner's Gary Cooper looks.

An emotive picture of Brian Leigh Exner, sitting alongside his older brother Virgil Jr, just months before the former's tragic death.

After the death of her son, Mildred was advised not to get pregnant straight away: this is Mildred and Bronwen aged just six weeks old almost one year to the day that Brian died.

when he and Mildred left the children in the capable hands of Mildred's mother and sister, and set off for a two-week vacation at a 'dude ranch'. Playing at cowboys, riding horses, and sleeping under canvas was a perfect tonic for the couple. Unfortunately, it was just a few weeks after they returned that tragedy struck the Exner family. On a warm August afternoon, the two young boys, Virgil Jr and his blond-haired two-year-old brother Brian, were playing upstairs at home in Virgil Jr's bedroom. Virgil left the room for a few moments, Brian climbed to the window and squeezed through the broken mesh blind that covered the open sash window. While trying to retrieve a small toy, he fell to the concrete path below and sustained severe head injuries. Mildred called an ambulance and asked them to meet halfway. She drove while Brian was held in his grandma's arms. That met the ambulance and rushed to Epsworth Hospital, in South Bend, then quickly transferred to University of Michigan Hospital in Ann Arbor, MI. His condition was serious but not thought to be life threatening. Although concussed, the following four weeks saw Brian make progress in his recovery before he was over-prescribed a new sulphur-based drug and penicillin, given because of a lung and kidney infection

he had contracted. The overdose caused his death in late September 1942. The family was devastated by the loss. Exner threw himself into his work as Mildred's family supported her in her grief. Although she was advised against it, Mildred fell pregnant in the fall of 1942 and suffered a traumatic nine months, mentally, and physically, but the Exners were delighted when she gave birth to a daughter, Bronwen Marie, on 28th June 1943. After the death of Brian, they wanted to move as soon as possible, and in April 1943 they bought a house on Eckman Street, and by August had sold the house on Long Island.

Virgil's interest in motor racing was not curtailed just because there was a war on, and in 1943 he stumbled on a dream. Whilst wandering around the Studebaker plant

This was how the 1932 Studebaker Indy race car looked before its subtle transformation into a road-going sportscar. It was capable of achieving 148mph, and covering the ¼ mile in 12.97 seconds at 108mph. Because of Ex's impending move to Chrysler in 1949, the car was sold to an aircraft engineer attached to the Wright-Patterson Air Force Base in Dayton, Ohio, before being bought back by Studebaker in 1952 and returned to its original configuration.

he discovered an Indianapolis race car that looked to still be in great condition. It was being stored one floor above his studio on the fourth floor of the engineering building. Studebaker had built a team of five cars for the 1932 Indianapolis race, with some success. In the 1932 race one came third and the following year the team placed all five cars in the top twelve. The cars were built by Herman Ringling, a race car builder of the time, with heavy input from Studebaker and used a 336in³ straight-eight Studebaker engine and chassis components. The engine was fitted with four Stromberg carburetors and offered 327 horsepower. It was a tremendous marketing tool for the company and, coincidentally, this was one of the cars

that a younger Virgil had illustrated whilst he was working for Advertising Artists.

After the 1933 race, the cars were retired and sold off to private individuals. This particular 2-seater car, and all of the Studebaker race team's spares, was sold to Phil Sanders, a plastics supplier also based in South Bend. He raced the car as the Sobenite (plastics) Special in the 1937 Indy 500, where it placed 10th, and then asked Studebaker to store it for him. Exner approached Mr Sanders, asking if he wished to part with the car. Sanders had all but forgotten the race car and agreed to sell it to Exner for the princely sum of $500. The price included the car and all of the spares. Over the next 12 months,

1932 Indy racer. Now with added head and taillights fitted, along with a rear-view mirror, dual folding windscreen, and license plate holder on the left-hand side and a bracket to mount a canvas suitcase under the right-hand exhaust headers, this was how Ex transformed a race car into a sportscar. He is seen here in 1947 with Les Taylor, owner of the so-called '1776 House' just outside of Avon, Connecticut, along with two Studebaker sales reps and a 1947 Champion. Taylor was an avid sportscar enthusiast, who regularly hosted the annual Sports Car Club of America meetings at his historic home.

Ex came up with a plan to make this Indy race car street legal. Road lights were added along with a rear-view mirror, dual folding windscreen, taillights, and license plate holder on the left-hand side and a bracket to mount a canvas suitcase under the right-hand exhaust headers, as well as a modified cast aluminum grille that he had designed. The car was then painted in black lacquer and trimmed in dark red leather, his favorite color combination. Once finished, and with lots of gasoline ration coupons saved, Exner, with his son Virgil Jr in the riding mechanics seat, filled the 20-gallon tank with high-octane gas and made several trips to the East Coast in the car between 1944 and 48. An embryonic post-war racing scene was developing and Exner was there at the beginning and was a member of the Sports Car Club of America alongside Briggs Cunningham and Russ Sceli. The SCCA let Exner join even though his car was a race car and not a sports car as they saw it. Virgil Jr remembers one such trip from just after the war. "We were loafing along at about 80mph – no speedo – the big 4½in tach was showing 2400rpm. We were eastbound for the SCCA summer event at Thompson, Connecticut. There was hardly any traffic. We were due to stop at Somerset for fuel; Dad was nursing it a bit as there was no [fuel] gauge to go by. I noticed that Dad started to pay more attention to his cowl-side rear view mirror a ways after Laurel Hill. I took a quick look back over the tail. 'It's a '41 Packard, Dad.' He nodded. I looked again, it was gaining. Dad applied a little more throttle. There was no speed limit in 1948 on the Pennsylvania Turnpike. I looked again in time to see the big, black four-door moving into the passing lane and that two gents wearing Homburg hats appeared to be sitting bolt upright. We were now doing close to 90. The straining Packard inched on by, the gents heads unturned, their noses lifted higher. They stretched the distance until returning to our lane. Dad lifted a little and fell back to 2300rpm, then BANG, BANG! He double de-clutched, shifted down into second and put his foot into it! The rear tires chirped, then bit, and the revs soared rapidly as engine and gears screamed! He switched to the passing

1944 Studebaker studio photo. 'The gang's all here'. Rear table: Vince Gardner, John Reinhart; next table: Jack (Jake) Aldrich, Frank Ahlroth; third table from back: Audrey Moore, Gordon Buehrig; fourth table: Holden 'Bob' Koto; front table: Bob Bourke, Virgil Exner; standing over model: Virginia Spence (facing camera), Nancy Spence. (Studebaker Museum)

lane and we pulled quickly alongside at 100. Pow! Pow! Dad put her in high! Again, the Firestones burned and we streaked ahead! I looked back to see the gents' mouths were agape. Dad wound it up to 4100, close to 137mph (the rev limit was 4500rpm) and held her there until we got to the Somerset exit sign. We parked, climbed out, removed our cloth helmets, and were taking off our kidney belts along with our World War II flying suits when the gents pulled in next to us. As usual, a few onlookers were gathering. The men got out and rushed over, doffed their hats and one said, 'What is that? What'll she do?!' Dad said to me 'Virgil ... ?' He always left it to me to explain. At the end of my explanation, the reaction was always the same. 'Really? ... Wow!' However, for me, the biggest thrill of the trip was that Dad actually let me drive 'our special'

on the track. I was 15. The loud pedal was more sensitive than I had ever imagined and Dad had to hang on for dear life for a change!" Both Exners would keep a keen interest in motorsport and, during the late 1940s, even crewed for racing driver Sam Hanks (1957 Indy winner) and others at Midget race meetings held in South Bend. Virgil Jr would go on to compete in local race meetings, behind the wheel of a 1927 Bugatti.

In 1943, war work continued apace but the green light was given to develop the post-war car, too. In an interview years later with author Michael Lamm, Exner explains: "Gene Hardig (chief chassis engineer) and I went to Roy Cole (engineering, Vice President) about this time, 1942-43, because neither of us was too busy with war projects. We sold him on the idea of letting us do an advanced design. This would be engineered to some degree toward production. We sold Cole on this, and I built a ¼-scale model. Soon after that we built a full-sized wooden mock-up in the Studebaker die-model shop. This was a flush-sided job, and that's what convinced me that the first post-war car shouldn't be completely flush-sided. It should have a pontoon rear fender because of the belt-line at the time. It seemed to have an awfully heavy look. But the upper structure, the curved windshield and the wraparound back window and rear deck – those turned out quite a bit like the post-war production car." Studebaker bosses were under the impression that Loewy was trying to take as long as possible with designs so as to inflate the expenses and they had an inkling that he was not fully committed to Studebaker alone due to his other contracts, so Loewy was falling from favour. Eager to get back into civilian production as soon as possible, Roy Cole, along with Studebaker President, Harold Vance, encouraged Virgil to set up a studio at the new Exner family home at 1120 East Eckman Street in South Bend. Cole wanted Ex to work on alternatives to the main studio designs in his spare time. It was no secret that Virgil was disenchanted with Loewy's managerial style and his habit of taking credit for his designers' work. Over the coming months Ex would come to bitterly despise Loewy and his slave-driver attitude towards his staff. He appreciated that designing a car was a team effort and he wanted that team to receive some of the glory, whereas Loewy expected to take full responsibility for all design success because it was his company. Feeling more obligated to his client than to his boss, and with a burning ambition to prove himself, Ex borrowed a couple of modelers (Fred Hornung and Vic Clark) and set up shop in his basement. In an interview years later, Ex recalled, "I agreed to start immediately. I first cleaned out one of my bedrooms at home – this was in the spring of 1944 – and they sent me out an 8ft drafting board. Then we went into the basement and installed an overhead fluorescent light, and built me a ¼-scale clay-modeling table down there. Gene Hardig, who was then chief of chassis drafting, came out every day. We worked on seating and chassis layouts. This was my job, then, to be worked on nights and weekends." Even the young Virgil Jr remembers helping his father by adding clay to the ¼-scale models when not working on his own designs. "I was always playing with the modelers that were there (that my Dad had come in, and were modeling the car). Fred and Vic had been in the service, and had served in the Pacific, and they were keeping track of the war. They had a map on the basement wall. They were young, only 19, 20 years old, and had been called, and already done their service time, and come back, during the war."

The result was two teams working on the same

A rare picture of the whole family together; Mildred, Virgil Jr, Bronwen and Virgil Sr on the steps of a memorial during a family vacation.

project. It has been rumored that Cole deliberately gave the Loewy designers false dimensions to work from and gave Exner the desired parameters, but Cole and Exner refuted this. By the time Exner saw the engineering outlines for the first time, the Loewy team had already started work on its designs. It didn't take long for Exner to come up with an alternative to what he saw developing in the studio. Ex did, however, persuade Cole to give a little on his stringent dimensions. The dimensions called for a family car with a wheelbase of 110in and a width of just 67in. Ex recalled, "Roy Cole had a thing – his philosophy was that a car cost so much a pound. He stuck to that rigidly, and these were the dimensions he laid down. They were a little tough to work with." Exner cajoled Cole into stretching the width to 70 inches and the wheelbase to a proportionate 113in. "The body drawings were simply opened up and a three-inch strip put down the center

Built in secrecy, this was the full-size mock-up of Exner's initial post-war Studebaker design. Once built, he decided against the heavy, slab-sided look and added pontoon rear fenders. Designed to be fitted with either a front or rear engine, the car featured a large greenhouse area and tri-star insignia, one of Loewy's favourite design touches.

without changing the profile, and the wheels moved back. Then the front end looked too short, I convinced Mr Cole that we should add three inches to the fenders and two inches to the hood." It was these modifications more than anything else that gave Exner the upper hand. Cynics have accused Cole of purposely not telling the Loewy team of the changes, but whether it was done intentionally or not, they were not given the modified dimensions. At one point, Studebaker considered building it as a rear-engine automobile, so a prominent grille ran across the back of the car. Engineers and stylists agreed it was worth looking into. Cole was familiar with Porsche's skill in building rear-engined vehicles so contracted it to build two prototype cars. The first was a rear-engine, rear-wheel drive car, and the other one was a front-engine, rear-wheel drive car. They were both

Already silver-haired, Ex works at a clay model in 1944 which closely predicts how the all-new post-war Studebaker would look.

deemed to be mechanically sound but the decision was taken to stay with the traditional front-engine, rear-wheel drive configuration.

Loewy tried to fly into South Bend once a week, but sometimes only managed once a month. It was his practice to call his offices every morning, including Manhattan, London, Paris and, of course, South Bend. On these irregular visits to Indiana, the tension between Exner and his boss increased. Exner's colleagues from this period have stated that although Ex was a fantastic man to work for, very mild and quietly spoken, he was not the kind of man who would forgive and forget very easily. The two men began to squabble heavily, to the degree that Loewy hired another chief designer, Gordon Buehrig. Buehrig had spent time with Harley Earl's Art and Color Section in the early thirties, and with Duesenberg in Indianapolis. It was Buehrig who designed the much revered Duesenbergs and Cords of the late 1930s and the beautiful 851/852 Auburn Speedster. Buehrig recalls, "I ran across a friend of mine by the name of Carl Otto who was an associate of Raymond Loewy Associates, and Loewy was building up a design department at Studebaker, and he hired me to head up this group and build up a larger department, and I hired some old friends like John Rhinehart, Jack Aldrich, Bob Koto. Virg had been there before I was, and Virg was my assistant, and then Loewy came out from New York one day and got mad at me and made Exner manager and made me his assistant. Then in another period he came out and fired Exner and put me in charge. I mean, it was a funny political situation."

Loewy instructed Buehrig to set up a separate design department, so he moved them across from the Sample Street building and took over the top floor of Building 48. Gordon's new intake of staff, including Dick Calleal and Vince Gardner (also from Duesenberg), carried on with designs for the first post-war car.

When Loewy was not in South Bend, Virgil and Gordon got on very well and became close friends; Gordon's first wife, Betty, became best of friends with Mildred Exner, and they often spent evenings out as a foursome. It made no difference to either of them who was in charge on a daily basis, work progressed as usual. In February 1944, Exner made history by employing the first ever female industrial designer, Audrey Moore (née Hodges). At a time when many of the traditional male jobs had been taken up by women as the male workforce went to war, the fledgling business of industrial design was still a male-dominated area. Gender was never an issue for Exner or any of the team there. Audrey recalls, "They didn't consider it at all, and I never felt the least bit unique, or uncomfortable, or anything. It was a job. I had assignments along with the men. Our assignments

were carried out, and I did the work the same as they did. In fact, how the designs would evolve would usually be when there was a meeting of the sales people, and engineers would all meet and say what we need to do is to revamp like a front end, or a back end, or a door section, or an instrument panel, or whatever, and 'we'll need some sketches by such and such a time'. Each one of us was given a number for our designs. They didn't go by name – we were given a number, so no one ever knew whose work they were judging." Although Loewy was not in South Bend very often, his presence was always felt. Years later, Audrey recollected that Exner "was just a very charming man and very easy to work for". As for Raymond Loewy, she says ,"He was always going around the studio, in fact, our whole building, tacking up signs that said, 'Weight is the Enemy', because materials had gone to war, and so we had all these signs to remind us that we must think small. 'Think small'. They wanted a shorter car, a smaller car; everything had to be smaller than previously because of the shortage of materials." The only other women there were two clay modelers, a mother and daughter, Virginia and Nancy Spence, who became close friends with Audrey.

Designs from both Exner's and Loewy's teams were being whittled down to just a few choices for the final selection and got as far as ¼-scale clay models . Many of the designers at Studebaker could use clay as well as the professional modelers. Virgil, Gordon, Bob Bourke and Bob Koto were all adept at modeling with the hot material. Bob Bourke remembers: "Ex would model, and I would model. On occasion, we would really get into the clay. With Frank [Alhroth], there was three of us. Clay in your shoes, and hands, and fingernails, and every piece of silver change in your pocket turned black with the sulphur." Always impeccably dressed in a sharp suit, Exner ruined many clothes with his enthusiasm for modeling.

The ¼-scale clay model that Virgil had been working on progressed to a full-sized mock-up built in Studebaker's die-model shop. This was all done in complete secrecy. When it was unveiled for Studebaker's bosses in late May 1945, they liked it; Loewy, however, did not. When he found out about the clandestine work that Exner and his modeler, Frank Alhroth, had been doing on the 1947 plans, his volatile temper exploded. In the first week of June 1945, he took the train from New York to Indiana so he could argue with Exner face-to-face. He quite rightly accused Exner of disloyalty and insubordination. Loewy is supposed to have shouted: "I will have nothing more to do with you, you are immediately fired!" Roy Cole, who was also present at this impromptu meeting, replied, "You are immediately hired, Mr Exner, by Studebaker Corporation."

Ex and Loewy together in the modeling studio. It was here that they had the argument which ended Ex's contract with Loewy, when Ex revealed the clay model that he had been working on at home.

Although upset by the confrontation and Loewy's action, Exner was not unduly disturbed by his sacking, as he knew that Roy Cole was as good as his word. The very next day, Cole hired Exner as Studebaker's Chief Styling Engineer. Loewy was incensed but could do little about it as the contract with Studebaker was still valuable and he was obliged to keep a design team there. What he did do, however, believing that Gordon Buehrig was in on the project Ex had ben working on, was fire him, too, and put Bob Bourke in charge of the Loewy team. Roy Cole set Exner up with an office at the proving grounds; Exner

hired Bud Kaufman, Ed Hermann and Randy Farrout, and worked alongside Studebaker engineer and best friend Dale Cosper, continuing to work on various designs for the post-war car with his new staff. The talented Cosper had also come from Duesenberg, and was instrumental in the development of Buehrig's famous Auburn Cord Duesenberg designs. This odd set-up continued until Loewy's contract ended in 1955, with two design teams in friendly competition with each other.

Cole hadn't quite finished playing around with the Loewy team, though. Almost as soon as they had become comfortable in Building 48, Cole threw them out of there and moved them to an automobile dealership – Sherman, Shaus and Freeman – three blocks away. Cole had one-third of the second floor of the building sectioned off and squeezed them in there. The Loewy designers, now led by Bob Bourke, had to walk through all the display cars and the workshop to get to the area. It was at this point that Cole may have played around with specifications and dimensions. Bourke reminisces, "We'd do a full-size clay model, then, if you can imagine this, we'd get at the last minute the fact that the car had to be 2 inches narrower. Okay, and somewhat shorter by 2 inches or 3 inches. 'And you can't show it unless it's in the right dimensions,' Roy Cole would say to me. 'Yes, sir, Mr Cole.' 'You'd better figure out what you're going to do, because the car's too big.' Then he'd stomp out of the place, and I'd say, 'Yes, sir, Mr Cole,' and scratch my head. So we'd take and we'd cut the plaster model. We had gone through the clay, and it was real nice, and it was just ready to be painted. You'd look at it and go around the thing. We'd take the plaster model and just take whatever we had to take out of it – two inches, three or four inches – and cut it, and then we'd put it together like this and then finish it off in the middle and redo the whole thing. And we'd do it in a matter of about three or four days just working night and day. Just unbelievable. Just crazy stuff."

As for the 1947 design, Exner's and Cole's plans to get the first post-war car into production succeeded.

The first post-war Stude' was initially a very mild face-lift of the 1942 models, released as the Skyway Champion, in three- and five-passenger coupe and two- and four-door sedan versions. They sold extremely well whilst the factory set up the tooling for the all-new car. Studebaker was in a better position than the big three in Detroit to get back into civilian production. Few workforce or union issues arose and, working on a smaller scale, retooling could be done much quicker, although still at an estimated $11 million to develop. The all-new car debuted in late autumn of 1946 as a 1947 model to a huge reception. The '47s were immediately popular with the buying public, although celebrated wits at the time quipped that they couldn't tell if the car was going backward or forward. This extra publicity was due to Exner's gently-curved one-piece front windshield and the dramatically curved three-piece rear windscreen that wrapped around almost to the doors on the two-door coupe version of the Champion and Commander. Compared to pre-war models, the new cars were a complete departure from standard design ideology of the time. It is not an exaggeration to say that Ex totally reshaped the modern American automobile and established the design pattern for all modern cars. They

Another Exner patent, this one showing a whole car; Ex's design for the Champion Starlight Coupe.

Vision produced this car of vision!

STUDEBAKER engineers and stylists knew you wanted a better view in back as well as in front when you're driving.

So they envisioned a car with panoramic windows all around—spent years in designing and redesigning it—came up with this dream-lined new Starlight Coupe!

Envied throughout the automotive world is this engineering resourcefulness! It underlies the extra vision—the deep-bedded riding comfort—the light-touch handling ease—of all the fabulously fine new Studebaker dream cars!

They're swung so low, the very law of gravity itself assures road-hugging stability without weave or wander.

They're the world's first cars with brakes designed to adjust themselves automatically! Brake servicing is seldom needed—there's a "like-new" pedal feel, mile after mile!

See them all! Champion and Commander sedans, coupes, convertibles—a special extra-long-wheelbase Studebaker Land Cruiser!

STUDEBAKER

First in style...first in vision...first by far with a postwar car © Studebaker Corporation, South Bend 27, Ind., U.S.A.

---

were lower, wider and sleeker looking than any non-luxury car built before. Ex had integrated the front fenders to make a full-width body, then brought the fenders forward to a position slightly proud of the front grille and lowered hood. During the cars' development, Exner had used ¼-scale models in the wind tunnels at the University of Michigan to ensure his designs were aerodynamic. Convertibles, sedans, and coupes were built for the 1947 model year but the runaway success was the 2-door Champion Starlight Coupe, which emphasized that neat wraparound rear end to perfection. In later years, many

designers, including Harley Earl himself, would cite Exner's 1947 design as a reference point for their own work.

Exner's team worked on the face-lift models and major re-designs for the next five years. The face-lifts were mainly ornamental changes and the development of the larger Land Cruiser. Although Bob Bourke claims responsibility, Exner was also involved with the Studebaker trucks and was particularly pleased with his work on the 1949 pick-ups. Exner's design philosophy of making cars that looked and drove like automobiles, not space rockets, led him into joining the SAE (Society of Automotive Engineers) and being invited to become the vice chairman of the ASBE (American Society of Body Engineers), high office indeed for someone with no recognized engineering training. Here he had the platform to preach his philosophy when he gave speeches at these organizations' conventions. In early June 1947, Virgil talked to the SAE members about where he saw the future of auto design going, blending science, engineering and art to create highway vehicles that were efficient and beautiful – making art practical. In that speech he lambasted other designers of the time, when he observed the lack of influence exerted by what Ex called 'Buck Rogers' automobile stylists.

During the war, the 'table-cloth artist, the air-brush expert and the plush scale model stylist' had designed covered-cockpit rocket-style cars that were totally impractical to build or use, on a cost as well as engineering basis. But one aspect that Ex did encourage was aircraft styling. He foresaw aircraft design having a powerful influence upon future car design, as automobiles became faster, and streamlining and noise would become ever more important factors. Losing structural irregularities and unwanted projections helped to streamline the

Now based in the proving grounds, Ex continued to design cars for Studebaker. These previously unpublished images show a small 100in wheelbase, two-door coupe featuring a hatch-type trunk that carries all the way up to the rear screen, enabling a huge amount of luggage space. If it had gone into production, it would have been built in a four-wheel drive configuration. After Ex left to work for Chrysler, the design was forgotten and this full-size wooden mock-up was destroyed.

automobile. He did not want automobiles to look like aeroplanes, however, but the aerodynamics behind their design was Exner's goal. A combination of beauty with function, producing a clean appearance, but a car still had to look like a car, first and foremost.

In November 1948, it was the turn of the ASBE to host Virgil Exner when he gave a similar speech, entitled 'Are Dangerous Curves Ahead?' In this talk, attended by many stylists, once again he attacked the Buck Rogers design philosophy and requested that designers

and engineers think hard about where automobile style was going. Would their efforts still look like the design's ultimate function – a mode of transport? He compared British, French and Italian schools of thought, offering that the English were too traditional and dated, the French designs were "fruity, effeminate and decadent, and the Italians a refreshing blend of modern smoothness with the classicism of a day long passed. And, the Italian car looks like an automobile." His concern was that the newly found sleekness and raciness of American cars would be sacrificed if current trends towards flights of fancy prevailed. Rather prophetically, he feared that the tendency towards bulkiness and fat contours could only lead to the loss of individuality, as all cars looked the same, a philosophy he described as the 'Big Package'.

Studebaker bought a Jowett Javelin over from England for analysis. It wanted to make an even smaller car than the Champion. Designed by a team led by Gerald Palmer, the Javelin had such advanced features as a flat-four push-rod engine, independent front suspension with torsion bars front and rear, and unitary body construction. Virgil Jr remembers driving the little tan-colored car around South Bend on numerous occasions and the family used it to get to the Milwaukee speedway on at least one occasion. On the basis of this little British car, Exner worked in complete secrecy, even from his friends in the Loewy gang, and came up with a design for a new small Studebaker. The design featured a sloping fastback rear end that worked like a modern hatchback. The deep parcel-shelf and long trunk lid that went up to the rear

screen, allowed a large amount of luggage to be packed. A full-sized wooden mock-up was built out at the proving grounds studio that had a detailed interior and exterior. It was a very well proportioned and good looking automobile but Studebaker bosses eventually decided that because the Champion was doing so well in a strong market, it was no longer required. The prototype was destroyed and the few staff that knew of its existence were sworn to secrecy. A few photos kept by Exner are all that is left of the design.

Of the cars that did see production, Exner didn't get it all his own way there either. The face-lift for the 1950 Studebaker called for a low hood-line plunging down between the new-style fenders, to meet a shallow, horizontal grille – Ex's interpretation of contemporary Italian Grand Tourer styling. It was Vince Gardner on the Loewy team who came up with the chrome encrusted aircraft nose for their submission for the 1950 models. Much to Exner's disgust, Studebaker bosses preferred that front grille over Exner's, so the final car that Ex worked on for

One benefit of working on your own, away from prying eyes, was the opportunity to create designs for yourself. This was Exner's proposal for an advanced mid-engined midget racing car, done while at Studebaker in March 1947.

Type R·E·25·
V.M EXNER MAR.'47

Studebaker was an amalgamation of work from both teams. As it turned out, the design was incredibly popular with the buying public and media alike.

On the home front, Mildred and Virgil paid attention to their growing family. On 29th August 1947, Mildred's sister Leola Weatherwax tragically died in childbirth but the baby survived. Leola's husband was found wanting of parenting skills so the Exners adopted June Marie into their family. The household was run by Mildred; it was she who taught the young Virgil Jr to drive at the tender age of thirteen, in the family's 1941 President. After working at the studio, Ex would always come home, play with the children, and look over their schoolwork. The family would then eat at 6:30 and discuss their day. Ex told his family about work, the politics, and the designs going on in the studio. The couple took a keen interest in whatever the children were doing, never missing parent-teacher meetings and school events. Because of their openness, the family was very democratic and the children were involved in decision making whenever possible. Once the children were in bed,

if he wasn't working on a design for Roy Cole, Virgil would listen to the radio and sometimes draw or went to bed relatively early and read. Ex and Mildred both liked to read romantic or detective novels. Mildred also enjoyed knitting as a way of relaxing. Ex had a low tolerance to alcohol and knew that it didn't take much to get drunk, but it didn't slow him down when he wanted to relax. In an interview with Dave Crippen of the Edsel Ford Design History Center, Bob Bourke states that Ex "was a hard-drinking guy. Holy smokes. Gosh, he was something else. As a young fellow, he was wild. But he was there on the job every morning bright and early, and he didn't ever walk, he ran from one place to another. He was just a real banger." It was the weekends that they would really let their hair down and would socialize with friends and relatives. They drank with their close friends like the Allens, the Hodgemans, Bourkes, Cospers, Buehrigs, the Kotos, and the Schafer family in South Bend, or Mildred's brothers and sisters from nearby Three Rivers, Michigan. Exner's favorite drink was a Manhattan made with ⅔ Canadian

Clay model 1944. This never-before-seen picture was taken in the basement of the Exner home on Eckman street, and shows Exner's ¼-scale clay proposal for the Tasco. When Buehrig bought out the other guys, he had Vince Gardner do a totally different design, which he presented as a finished ¼-scale model.

George W, Virgil Sr, and Virgil Jr attending a family wedding.

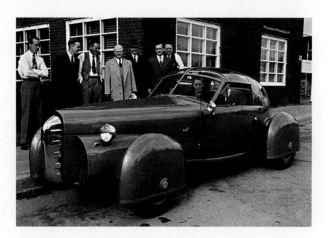

The Tasco prototype sportscar, started off as a home project in Exner's garage. Based on a modified Mercury chassis, Gordon Buehrig took over the project and developed it into this. The Tasco was originally powered by a modified 1948 Mercury engine. Modifications included an Edlebrock dual intake manifold with twin Holley 94 carburetors. Decorative Thickstun head covers were also fitted. Built of post-WWII aluminum, it was shown unsuccessfully in Wichita in 1948 in the hope of contracting with Beech Aircraft Company for production of the aviation-inspired automobile. Shown here at the Cardwell Manufacturing Company in Wichita. The Tasco is now owned by the Cord Auburn Duesenberg Museum in Auburn, Indiana.

Club whiskey, ⅓ sweet red vermouth, a dash of bitters, and a red cherry. He had his own slight variation, and even filed marks on a cocktail shaker glass so that it would always get precise measurements. Mildred would always keep an eye on the quantity that Virgil was consuming and discretely let him know.

Exner Sr's close relationship with his work colleagues lead to a private enterprise away from Studebaker. Ex liked to work at home in his own studio, and, if he wasn't drawing race cars or dreaming up projects, he was working on fine art. He, along with Gordon Buehrig, Bob Bourke and Dale Cosper, went in together on a 'home' project. Exner junior recalls that between them, they went to a local junkyard in South bend and bought a 1939 Mercury chassis and started to design and build a sports car in the Exner garage. With Dale doing the welding, they shortened and 'Z'ed the chassis and moved the engine back. Meanwhile, Ex was working on a small-scale clay model of what he thought the car should look like, and Gordon and Bob did the same. The car was initially planned to be made of fiberglass because of Cosper's extensive knowledge of the process. Cosper left Studebaker and, with money staked by Ex, he bought some aircraft tooling and pipe bending equipment and started to make a tubular frame for the car. Interestingly, he used this same equipment to develop a successful seat for women to shampoo their hair, and a wheelchair, becoming the largest manufacturer of wheelchairs in America before going into golf buggy production.

The close-knit team came up with a car that Gordon Buehrig went on to develop. After Loewy had fired Buehrig, the designer was at a loose end. Coincidentally, a group of industrialists were looking for a car to be used for European-style grand prix racing in New York State. They set up The American Sports Car Co, in Hartford, Connecticut which resulted in the Tasco. Gordon bought out the others in the team and had Vince Gardner create a ¼-scale model of his design. In the end, the body was made from aluminum and powered by a modified 1948 Mercury engine with Edlebrock dual intake manifold and twin Holley 94 carburetors. The engine was later fitted with an Ardun overhead valve conversion, and remains in that configuration today. The car featured streamlined wing-like fenders, a glass aircraft-style canopy, and lift-off roof panels. The unusual wheel fairings did cause unresolved steering problems. Although it is rumored that Buehrig was never satisfied with the design, from this car came the design for a T-top, which eventually became the removable T-top for Thunderbird and Corvette. Once completed, the Tasco was shown in Wichita, Kansas, late in 1948 in the hope of entering into a contract with Beech Aircraft Company for production of the aviation-inspired automobile. Walter H Beech and his wife, Olive Ann

One of the last designs that Ex worked on before leaving Studebaker was this coupe, drawn in 1948. This was one of three proposals for the 1950 model year. Note the bullet nose front grille. (Brett Snyder)

Beech, owners of the company, declined the offer and the idea went no further. The only Tasco made survives and is now on display at the Auburn-Cord-Duesenberg Museum in Auburn, Indiana.

Roy Cole, Exner's major corporate benefactor, was due to retire at the end of 1949 and, understanding the nature of business politics, he was worried that Virgil's position at Studebaker would become untenable once he had gone. So, in the fall of 1948, whilst work on the 1950 models was being finalized, Cole started to contact friends in the business to see if he could find another position for his chief styling engineer.

One of the first people Cole spoke to was John Oswald, executive engineer at Ford Motor Company and the man in charge of body engineering and styling. Cole told Oswald that Exner was available and asked if he would be interested in hiring him. Oswald replied, "Yes, I would be very interested", so Ex went to Detroit

and had a meeting with him. Virgil Jr states that Oswald made a verbal agreement with Exner, telling him, "Come up and look for a house, and you will become chief designer of Ford." With the promise of a huge increase in income, the family went to Detroit several times on house hunting expeditions and finally found a plot they liked and committed to buying a beautiful home North of Detroit in Bingham Farms. Ex was very excited about this move, not only because of the sharp increase in pay, and the chance to be rid of Loewy, but many of his friends and ex-colleagues already worked in the design department at Ford. But on 8th April 1949, Oswald dropped a bombshell on the Exners when he wrote to Virgil stating he was going to renege on his agreement, the policy committee had decided to hire George Walker instead. Virgil was bitterly disappointed, his artistic ego taking a large dent, but when he told Roy Cole about the situation Cole just replied, "Well ok, let's try Chrysler".

When Walter P Chrysler retired in July 1935, he left the corporation in a strong position, even though it was reeling from the dramatic failure of the Airflow. The hasty replacement, the Airstream models, were styled by Phil Wright at Briggs Manufacturing Company, and toned down the Airflow design, giving them a modern, attractive look without so much streamlining. Popular cars indeed, so when Chrysler handed the reins over to his second-in-command, Kaufman Thuma (K T) Keller, and his two lieutenants B E Hutchinson (treasurer) and Fred M Zeder (engineering), he thought he was leaving the corporation in good hands. By 1949, however, things were not looking so rosy. Keller admitted that he was 'a machinist by trade'. Excellent at production management, styling was not his forte. His insistence that buyers of Chrysler Corporation cars should be able to wear their hats inside the cars kept the models boxy and staid. Hutchinson held the purse strings and was giving very little to research and development. Chrysler Corporation's envied reputation as an engineering leader was having less influence on the buying public as competitors released exciting new post-war models. The media had a field day, proclaiming doom and gloom for the company. *Fortune* magazine correctly predicted in October 1948 that Chrysler's 1949 models would be dull, if well-engineered. Ford released its 'all-new for 1949' models and knocked Chrysler from the number two position in the corporate manufacturer's league. In a period when there was an unprecedented demand for personal transportation, Chrysler's production totals were increasing slowly year on year, but the market share was dropping rapidly. Even the stubborn K T saw that something had to be done.

Roy Cole was a friend of fellow engineer James (Jim) C Zeder, Chrysler's Director of Engineering and Research, and younger brother of Fred Zeder. Cole phoned Jim, informing him that Exner would soon be available. At that time, Chrysler had only a small styling section controlled mainly by engineers. Even before Cole's timely phone call, there had been talk of setting up an advanced styling studio to look into the corporation's future designs. Jim Zeder spoke directly to Keller and they both agreed this was a great opportunity. Keller was very aware of Exner's accomplishments at Studebaker and enthusiastically agreed to meet the designer. Virgil travelled to Detroit once more. The meeting in August of 1949 went well; Keller

officially offered Ex the post of Chief of the Advanced Styling Studio, a department that did not as yet exist but would be created for and by Virgil Exner. Exner looked upon this as a demotion, but also a means to an end. The Chrysler position offered $25,000 per year, half the salary that Ford had promised and no input into any of the production models; this was still going to be controlled by Chrysler's corporate design chief and Ex's immediate boss, Henry King, and K T Keller of course.

So the Exners were on the move again, this time to 1036 Westwood Drive in Birmingham, a leafy suburb north of Detroit Central and off of Woodward Avenue. Their five bedroom home was built for them on a plot of land that they had bought. The colonial style building held a large studio at the rear for Ex's work. Whilst the Westwood

K T Keller, seen here with a model of one of his favored boxy cars, is blamed for Chrysler Corporation's bland styling through the forties and into the fifties. He was, however, instrumental in hiring and empowering Exner to change Chrysler's styling.

Exner's first task at Chrysler was to create a fresh new parade phaeton. Three were built and presented in 1952 to the cities of New York, Los Angeles and Detroit. The last one was intended for the White House but it refused the gift.

Drive house was being constructed, the family lived in rented accommodation. Once they had moved into their own home, Virgil Jr was enrolled into the exclusive Cranbrook School in nearby Bloomfield Hills as a boarding student, and Bronwen attended Quarton Elementary School in Birmingham. June (called Marie) was only two years old at this time and stayed at home with Mildred. On joining Chrysler, he sold his Studebaker race car and took advantage of his position to buy a new Chrysler. His choice was a new dark red 1949 Chrysler Windsor Highlander four-door, which he described as "a nice,

solid, comfortable clunker". His other car, a Tulip Cream 1949 Champion convertible, was then used exclusively by Mildred until 1954, when she gave it to Virgil Jr.

Ex, now aged 40, was set up in relative isolation from the production stylists, in his own studio in the Engineering Building at Highland Park, and although he described this period as "solitary confinement", he enjoyed working on his own in a separate studio. Some of his colleagues would later describe the silver haired stylist (Ex had gone prematurely grey, then silver by the time he started at Chrysler) as secretive, reclusive, and even unapproachable. But since his days with Studebaker, this genuinely shy man had been used to working in his own space, at home and at work, so this could be seen as a natural continuation of that practice. Exner was not without help. Because the production team only numbered seventeen at that time and none could be spared, he was given the go-ahead to employ new staff, a team of five, including a draftsman, modelers and stylists joined Ex in the 'isolation ward'. Talented Clifford C Voss came from Kaiser-Frazer to become Virgil's second-in-command, and they were ably assisted by Maurice (Maury) F Baldwin, Ted Pietsch, and modeler Harry Peterson. Reporting directly to Keller, Ex and his team were given three main tasks; design a parade phaeton, create a series of concept, or what Ex would call 'idea cars', and work on ideas that could be used on future production vehicles. Keller was looking for public support but more importantly, wanted to prove to potential investors and financial supporters that Chrysler could build exciting vehicles. He told Exner, "I want you to design the most beautiful car you can. It doesn't have to be a Chrysler, a Plymouth, a Dodge, a De Soto, or an Imperial; it just has to be beautiful." This was a prolific period for the designer, producing some of his most admired and creative works, but no easy task. His biggest problem would be to overcome the resentment that filtered over from the stylists already there and the overt hostility of the engineers that had thus far controlled design. Although talented Henry King was the Chief Designer, he answered to and did the beckoning of the Chief Engineer. It would take some time, but Exner's naturally amiable personality would win over in the end.

Three parade phaetons were built as a publicity exercise for Chrysler. Chrysler had created parade phaetons for the World's Fair for 1939 and 1940, hence the specifications for the new Phaetons mostly dated back to 1939, and were originally submitted by Grover Whalen, the official greeter for New York City. K T Keller wished to update the idea with modern looking vehicles, and once completed, they would be presented to New York, Los Angeles and the White House in Washington DC. Harking back to the days of the classic 1931 Imperial dual-cowl phaetons, Exner and Voss kept the design simple and elegant. The phaetons were built in Chrysler's own prototype workshop section, on a Crown Imperial Limousine chassis that was stretched 2in to achieve a wheelbase of 147.5in. To ensure Chrysler identity, a stock 1951 Imperial grille along with front and rear bumpers were used, but the rest of the all-steel metal body was completely unique. The low-slung fuselage (the height of the car from ground to cowl was just 45in) had a simple ridge running ¾ of the length of the body, ending in a kick-up rear fender bulge. The only ornamentation on the cars,

except for the Chrysler nameplates, was an Imperial eagle hood ornament. Being dual-cowl phaetons, front and rear passengers sat in separate compartments, each with its own curved windshield. There were no side windows, and the lightweight convertible top only covered the rear compartment. In keeping with the flowing design, the soft-top retracted fully beneath the rear-hinged deck lid when not in use, and the doors had no exterior handles.

Exner freely admitted that he was in love with the wheel, "one of man's oldest and most vital inventions, and also one of the purest and most beautiful. It is the essence of functional automotive design." The 1952 phaetons, as with most of his other designs, featured open but stylish wheelarches, showing off another Exner proclivity, large diameter wire wheels – yet another racing inspired styling keynote. Under the custom bodywork, the mechanics were standard top-of-the-line Chrysler for the period, a 180bhp, 331.1in³ FirePower Hemi V8 (with modified air cleaner to fit under the lower hood); full-time Hydraguide power steering, Ausco-Lambert disc brakes, Ori-flow shock absorbers and Fluid Torque transmission in which a torque converter replaced the usual Fluid Drive coupling. As Keller had planned, two of the vehicles were given to the cities of New York and Los Angeles. The third, the 'White House' car, did not make it to Washington. An official government reply stated that the White House was not permitted to receive gifts of that nature, so Chrysler titled the car within Detroit and shipped the car around at its discretion. The original color schemes were black with grey interior for New York, cream with red interior for LA, and green with tan interior for Detroit. The New York car made it to the big screen when it appeared in the 1953 movie *How to Marry a Millionaire* as Lauren Bacall's character Schatze Page arrives at an apartment building in it at the beginning of the film. All three cars have carried an almost endless list of the great and not so great, that reads like a *Who's Who*: Eisenhower, Kennedy, Johnson, Nixon, Winston Churchill, Haile Selassie, King Paul and Queen Frederika of Greece, Nikita Khrushchev, Governor Adlai Stevenson, General James Van Fleet, Colonel John Glenn and the crew of Apollo 11, and countless other senators, governors, mayors, ambassadors and movie stars. The cars initially remained the property of Chrysler, which serviced them, and in 1955, after three years of service, the cars were brought back to the factory and updated to 1956 Imperial appearance, in which form they continue to work to the present day. The front and rear, including grilles, bumpers and trim, were replaced. Mechanically, the engines were updated with 4-barrel carburetors, and fully automatic PowerFlite transmissions were installed. After the rebuild, the cars were permanently donated to the respective cities.

Exner and his small team of stylists had moved onto

In 1950, K T Keller commissioned Ghia to build a car to show its workmanship. The result was the Plymouth XX500. Not a winner in the styling stakes, but a neat little car nevertheless, and more importantly, beautifully put together. This would be the precursor to all the other Chrysler Ghia show cars up to the 1960s. Inspecting the car are, from left, Designer Henry King, H E Chesebrough (Chief Body Engineer), Robert Anderson (Chief Plymouth Engineer), John P Mansfield and R C Somerville (Vice President and General Sales Manager for Plymouth). (Ford Archive UK)

their next task, the first in a series of 'idea cars', when they were called down to the engineering garage by Keller. What he had to show them pleased Exner immensely. In 1950, after meeting company chiefs at the Turin Motor Show, Keller commissioned two of those companies to design and build one car each on a standard Chrysler chassis, supplied by Chrysler Export Vice President C B (Cecil Benton) Thomas. Both Italian coach builders, Pinin Farina and Carozzeria Ghia of Turin, tendered sample cars. Cliff Voss states that Keller really did not care how the cars looked but more over, how well they were built. When Ex and his team joined Keller to scrutinize the two new arrivals, it quickly became apparent that although both cars were well built, the Ghia (which was later named the Plymouth XX500) was by far the better-made vehicle. Keller told Ex that the Ghia had cost just $10,000 to

build, compared to the $83,000 just spent on each of the phaetons. This astounding difference in price, as well as the very high build quality, sealed the deal. Ghia would build the bodies for Exner's 'idea cars', starting with the current project, the K-310. With Exner's love of most things Italian, this was good news.

Carozzeria Ghia Spa was established 1921 in Torino (Turin) by Giacinto Ghia and Gariglio as Carozzeria Ghia & Gariglio, located at 4 Corso Valentino, Torino. The company specialized in bespoke coach building and design. Between the world wars, Ghia designed special bodies for Alfa Romeo, Fiat, and Lancia, one of the most famous was the Fiat 508 Ballilla sports coupe of 1933. The factory was demolished in an Allied bombing raid in 1943. Giacinto Ghia had just started to supervise the rebuilding of the site when he was taken ill and died of

Exner's first idea car was the Chrysler K-310, a five-passenger sport coupe that embodied the best of American and Italian design flair. The rear of the car featured a counter-balanced mounting that allowed the spare wheel to be raised from the trunk floor to a near vertical position, and those famous machine gun taillights, later dubbed microphone taillights. (Ford Archive UK)

heart failure on 21st February 1944. Determined that the family name would continue, Ghia's widow Santina offered the remnants of the company to two of his closest friends: Giorgio Alberti and Felice Mario Boano. So that their work could be readily shipped across Europe and abroad, Boano decided that a new location was required so the operation moved to Via Tomasi Grossi, nearer the railway station. It was Boano that Keller had spoken to at the 1950 Turin Motor Show and who had styled the XX500 sample car. To handle the newly-forged links with Chrysler, Boano brought in Luigi 'Gigi' Segre, an astute, enthusiastic 30-year-old designer, engineer and businessman. Soon after Ghia received approval of the sample car, Segre and Boano flew to Detroit. Even before their first meetings in America, the problem of translation reared its head as Boano spoke no English and Segre was just learning. Exner came to the rescue when he persuaded Paul Farago, an Italian-American friend he knew from racing, to interpret for the visitors. At that time Farago ran a specialty sportscar shop on the outskirts of Detroit, but soon became a full-time consultant for Chrysler and Ghia. The meeting went well with Segre, Farago, and Exner hitting it off straight away. In Exner, Segre had found a visionary with aspirations that could, and eventually would, make the alliance between the two companies one of the most significant of the post-war era, and help build Ghia's worldwide reputation, while Farago would become Ghia's US sales representative.

It was 1950, and work on the K-310 design had continued to the point that a ⅜-scale clay model was made. A plaster copy of this model was securely packed in a wooden case, ready for shipping to Italy, along with matching scale drawings. Unfortunately, by the time the crate arrived in Turin, the model was in pieces, so Boano relied on the draught plans. Major differences can occur when transferring detail from drawing to model, so when the project had reached the point where a full-size wooden mock-up had been created, Exner flew out to Turin to inspect and approve the work. What he found as he entered the courtyard simply amazed him; ancient stone sheds enclosed an old cobblestone courtyard and in the center sat the wooden car, built in 10in sections and with a mirror glass finish. Inside the structure, wood still had bark attached to it. His biggest surprise was the old craftsmen that he imagined working on his car were in fact little more than children, teenagers of 16, 17 and 18 years of age, very gifted and very fast. Around the courtyard stood old tree stumps, shaved to various curves and shapes and used as bucks. Exner watched in awe as the young men would take 10x10in pieces of steel and their hammers, look at the wooden model then beat the metal into shape over the tree stumps. They then walked over to the relevant part of the wooden mock-up and it would fit perfectly. Others would weld these small pieces together and once cooled, again a smooth contour would appear. The young workforce seemed undaunted if changes were required and affected these within hours. The Italians were good hosts and this first trip to Turin helped cement Segre and Exner's friendship, giving Ex the chance to buy some more of his much treasured fine Italian silk suits. He did feel that not all was well between Boano and Segre, with a definite atmosphere pervading their meetings. Only time would tell.

Given a free hand, the K-310 gave Exner the opportunity that he had been waiting for, a showcase for the design philosophy he had been promoting since his days at Studebaker. Simple, classic surfaces with minimal ornamentation, accentuating functional elements of the car instead of hiding them – elements like the wheels, radiator grille, spare tire, and lights. Clever two-tone (black on top, deep red on the body) paintwork integrated the upper and lower body, enhancing the optical impression of a lower, longer car. Circles were the keynote and were used extensively on the interior design. The grille design came directly from a sketch Ex had

A posed publicity shot of Luigi Segre and Ex with the 1952 K-310. Ex was used by Chrysler as a marketing tool, and by the mid-1950s had almost pop star status.

53

done earlier in 1951 for an open two-seat race car. The large wire wheels were housed in radiused wheelarches and the rear of the car featured the imprint of the spare wheel, which was originally planned to go under the trunk lid, and those famous 'gun-sight' taillights. The inspiration for those lights, generally known as 'mircophone' lights, came from machine gun-sights that Ex saw during the war. Given the prefix 'K' for Keller's involvement, and 310 for the hoped for horsepower (the actual 331in^3 FirePower Hemi V8 used gave 180bhp), the subtle blend of American and simpler Italian sportscar design created a classic coupe that looks as fresh today as it did when it was released on the 5th November 1951.

Being at Chrysler gave Exner the chance to purchase a car from a manufacturer that he much admired, but it wasn't a Chrysler. The designer managed to buy a black Mercedes-Benz 300 four-door sedan that had been bought by Chrysler Engineering for analysis, paying $1900 for it. Virgil Jr remembers, "Father had always wanted to own a Mercedes more than any other of the very few makes he cared about. Father and mother both enjoyed its beautiful, quiet ride and surprisingly good performance and handling. Black was his favorite color car. He kept it at home most of the time,

reserved for family trips. He sold it when he gained notoriety for his Chrysler 'idea cars'".

Evolving from the K-310 and arriving in quick succession were a series of similar 'idea cars', starting with the C-200, the 1952 Chrysler Special, the GS-1, the Thomas Special and the D'Elegance, all built by Ghia on Chrysler frames. All variations on a theme, the first draughts of these cars were done by Exner at home, in his purpose-built studio, and then refined at Highland Park. To cope with this heavy workload, Exner started building his design staff up to about thirty people. He conceded that he had little or no business or administration acumen, so he was pleased when he was allowed to hire some administrative personnel; this left him time to get back to the boards and do what he loved best, drawing cars.

The 1952 C-200 was a five-seat convertible

Exner tried to develop the theme of the K-310. Here we see two alternative proposals for a sportscar. The two-seat roadster and five-passenger coupe typify his love of the wheel and ways to accentuate it. (From the collections of The Henry Ford)

Exner's patent for the machine gun tail lamp as fitted to the K-310 and C-200, filed on 2nd December 1952. In modified form they would be used on production Imperial vehicles.

54

The K-310 was swiftly followed by the 1952 C-200, a convertible version of the hard-top coupe. This picture shows Luigi Segre (right) and Mario Boano on a barge in Genoa, Italy, awaiting transfer of the C-200 to the ocean liner, ready for its trip across the Atlantic. Segre accompanied the C-200 to New York and was present when dockers accidentally dropped the car onto American soil. Luckily, the car suffered only minor damage and, once fixed, could be shown on the motor show circuit.

Chrysler C-200.

The 1952 Chrysler Styling Special made its debut to the public at the Paris Auto Show of that same year. It was built on a shortened New York Chassis and powered by a 331in³ Hemi V8 engine producing 235 horsepower. It had power steering, brakes, windows and antenna. This three-passenger coupe was the only short-wheelbase version produced, and featured a sloping fastback and a flip-down spare wheel compartment behind the rear number plate housing. This picture, taken in Paris, shows the car in its original crème paintwork before being repainted in metallic green with a light green lower section.

version of the K-310 with no other major alterations, and was based on drawings and models sent by Chrysler. On completion, Segre accompanied the car on its cruise to America on the SS Constitution, this time without Boano. The C-200 had an ignominious arrival however. During unloading at New York docks the precious vehicle was dropped onto the quayside, much to the alarm of onlookers from Chrysler as well as Segre. Fortunately, damage was minimal and the car was able to join the circuit of motor shows around the country. Teasingly, Chrysler advertised this car as a prototype with hints that this was the direction that Chrysler was going with its next convertibles.

Still in 1952, the collaboration with Ghia offered the Chrysler SS (Styling Special), known as the Special. The elegant two-door sport coupe was unveiled at that year's Paris Auto Show to much acclaim. Sitting on a shortened 119in wheelbase New Yorker chassis, the Special and its longer 1953 namesake were built very much with European car buyers in mind. It is important

to remember that until this time, no American designer had ever influenced Italian style. Decades before the term 'world-car' was born, Exner and Segre were building the first. The classic long hood and short deck fitted perfectly to Exner's design. The slightly blistered fenders, front and rear, ran effortlessly into the main body and the gently sloping curve of the rear windscreen into the trunk was perfection. A panel between the trunk lid and rear bumper flipped down to reveal and release the spare wheel. The longer (125.5in chassis) 1953 version added a more conventional fastback with a more steeply-sloped rear windscreen to allow for more room inside. A functional air scoop adorned the hood, allowing the 331in³ Hemi V8 engine to breathe more easily. Fully engineered, the Specials also had the new Chrysler full-time power steering, electric windows and power brakes, and the '53 Special came with PowerFlite fully automatic transmission.

1952 Chrysler Special. The Chrysler Styling Special (or SS) was labelled the "sensation of the show" by the French press when it debuted in Paris in 1952. A superior blend of European styling, along with Exner's fundamental automotive design cues, created a timeless masterpiece.

Another one of these cars was built in 1953 specifically for a friend of Segre, Chrysler Export Division President C B Thomas. Exner met Thomas for the first time on a visit to France in early 1953 and agreed to Thomas' request to design and build a car just for him. Simply called the Thomas Special, at Thomas' suggestion, the car was to seat four adults comfortably, so it was based on the full-size New Yorker chassis. The coupe featured fully-radiused wheelarches, knock-off wire wheels, and vertical bumper guards that formed the

The Chrysler Special from 1952 was followed by another Special for 1953. Built on a longer 125.5in chassis, the '53 Special featured a more conventional rear end and trunk lid, allowing for more passenger space. Observant enthusiasts might notice the lack of a grille outline molding on the 1953 versions, and a more pronounced air intake on the hood.

The Thomas Special was built at the request of Chrysler's Export Division manager C B (Cecil Benton) Thomas. He loved the look of the Specials but wanted ample seating for four adults. Ex designed this car and, once again, it was built by Ghia. The most noticeable difference from other Specials was the split two-piece front windscreen.

The interior of the 1953 Special shows the standard of craftsmanship that went into each and every Ghia-built car.

leading edges of the front fenders and held the sidelights. Except for some minor trim details, the only other difference was that the Thomas had a split front screen whereas the previous 'Specials' had a one-piece curved screen and the spare wheel had a more conventional stowage space. Over the next few years, Ghia built eighteen more Thomas Specials, all of the same design but with one-piece curved windscreens.

The success of the Specials prompted a small production run by Ghia of the GS-1 coupe, a car inspired by Exner's earlier cars but with a modified front end. Four hundred were built between 1953 and 1954 and were sold exclusively in Europe by Societe France Motors, Chrysler's French business partner and distributor. As with the previous Ghia-built Chryslers, they were built atop a Chrysler 125.5in chassis, and were powered by a 180 horsepower version of the Chrysler FirePower Hemi V8 engine. The vehicles were equipped with either a Fluid Torque transmission or the newer PowerFlite two-speed automatic. Ex made his first appearance in *True* magazine, when Fawcett Publications released its first *True's Automobile Yearbook* in 1952. In an eight-page article, he mapped out the bloodlines of automobile styling from its inception to the 1950s, throughout Europe and North America.

Amongst all of this work, he still found time to visit Ghia in Turin, sometimes mixing business with pleasure and attaching the family holiday to the end of his business trips. This allowed the whole family to visit Italy and the rest of Europe. As the family travelled around in a car borrowed from Segre, Ex would try and locate ancient monuments and castles, doing a quick sketch that he could expand on when he returned home. Marie Exner told me that whilst they were in his favorite European city, Paris, he would rouse the whole family at just after 6am so that they could see as much as possible. Suffice to say this didn't go down too well with his twelve and sixteen-year-old daughters or the rest of the family, but his childlike enthusiasm was contagious. He and Mildred would spend

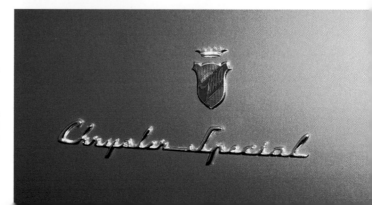

Often confused with the Thomas Special, Ghia produced eighteen more Specials, almost identical to the Thomas version but with a one-piece curved screen. Because of their relative rarity, survival rates are high. This one is on show at the Walter P Chrysler Museum in Detroit.

The success of the Specials prompted a small production run by Ghia of the GS-1 coupe, a model inspired by Exner's earlier cars but with a modified front end, featuring Chrysler New Yorker bumpers, restyled grille, and separate turn signals below the main headlamps. Four hundred were built between 1953 and 1954 and were sold exclusively in Europe by Societe France Motors, Chrysler's French business partner and distributor. As with the previous Ghia-built Chryslers, they had Chrysler 125.5in chassis, and were powered by a 180 horsepower version of the Chrysler FirePower Hemi V8 engine.

a lot of time on the Left Bank, haunting various bookshops and art galleries. The romantic in him searched out items on heraldic history, castles, Knights of the Round Table and Joan d'Arc in particular. In 1952, Ex received his first company car – a 1953 Chrysler New Yorker convertible fitted with a Hemi V8 and fluid-drive semi-automatic gearbox. The car was painted cream with a black top, and being Ex's, of course came with wire wheels. This was one of the first production Chryslers to receive any of his styling touches. From that time onward, he was allowed two production cars per year, many of which came with special paint and trim. Virgil Jr remembers: "Mother's car was usually a Plymouth with a special paint job and fitted cosmetics, etc. One year her Plymouth was painted in Westwood Blue, a new color named after the street we lived on in Birmingham, Michigan. It was very light, almost white in fact, and it became a production color the next year." Along with these company cars, Ex was allowed unlimited use of the 'idea cars' that he had designed once they had finished their corporate display duties.

Ex was trying to create a show car for each division to present through the 1954 season, but not all of the early 'idea cars' were styled by Ex and his team. Ghia came up with several concepts over the years, all based around an Exner car, but designed by Segre or Boano. The most noteworthy of these were the 1954 Plymouth Explorer and the 1953 Firearrow roadster. The Explorer was a smoothly-

The whole family was car crazy. This is Marie Exner outside the family home in Birmingham, MI, in 1951 enjoying her new pedal car. Ex customised the paintwork with pinstriping, the number 4 on the hood and fenders to signify her birthday, and a capital M above the grille.

Ex had been friends with Briggs Cunningham since 1944 so it was no surprise that Briggs asked Ex to design some proposals for a coupe and convertible race car to carry his new Chrysler Hemi engine. Although neither of these designs was used in its entirety, many of the styling cues seen in these sketches were used in later Cunningham C-3 and C-4 models in 1952 and 1953.

Plymouth did get a Ghia-built show car in 1954, the Explorer. As with previous 'idea cars' from this period, the Explorer was a neat two-passenger sport coupe that accentuated its sculpted lines by using little chrome ornamentation. Based on a 1954 Plymouth chassis and powered by the 230.2ci L-head 6 mated to a Hy-Drive semi-automatic clutch, the car radiated elegance and style. The exhausts exited through the rear fenders just below the rear lights. Matching suitcases were stowed in a leather-trimmed compartment.

The interior of the Explorer was trimmed in white leather with black accents, including the two bucket seats and center console. Retractable radio controls were hidden behind a moveable instrument panel to the right of the four main gauges. This photo was taken in Turin just after the car was completed.

The Dodge Firearrow was designed and built by Ghia following guidelines laid down by Virgil Exner. The engine-less, full-sized mock-up, seen here at the Turin Auto Show in 1953, carried very little ornamentation with just a Dodge shield on the hood and Firearrow nameplates on each front fender. The windshield was a raked-back, one-piece, unframed screen made of strengthened glass. The side molding that encompassed the body was painted metallic grey, contrasting with the bright metallic red bodywork. Note the quad headlamps, a first for Chrysler, that would go on to become an industry standard. (Ford Archive UK)

styled two-passenger sport coupe built on a conventional 1954 Plymouth chassis, and finished in bright metallic green with contrasting horizontal ivory-colored side moldings. The body design echoed other Ghia cars of the time but this show car had more sculpted fenders; the rear fenders could almost be described as fins. Beneath those tentative fins were neat taillight housings that also held the exhaust ports. The Firearrow was a non-working full-size body mock-up, which developed through a

series of fully-engineered Firearrow show cars into the 1954 Dodge Firebomb. The Firebomb itself became the prototype for the limited production Dual-Ghia.

Eugene A Casaroll was an American-Italian businessman who had set up Dual-Motors during World War II to build trucks and generators for the military, and

Two more Firearrow cars were built in 1954. The first was this two-seater sport coupe, which used a distinctive upper structure and an evolutionary front end. Unusual vents were built into the roofline just above the front windshield. The concave vented grille sat between cowled quad-headlamps and bumperettes. It was in this car that female racing driver Betty Skelton set a new closed-circuit world speed record for women when she topped 143.44mph at Chrysler's new Chelsea Proving Grounds. The car is now part of the Bortz collection. (Joe Bortz)

who also ran Automobile Shippers, Inc, Chrysler's main car transporter. Casaroll was smitten with the Firearrow IV roadster and approached Dodge Division's general manager, William Newberg, for permission to build the car. The rights were given and Newberg agreed to supply running chassis for the project. Casaroll asked close friend Paul Farago to re-engineer the Firearrow IV for production. Working with Ghia, Farago created the Dodge Firebomb prototype, which was unveiled to the public at the 1955 Geneva Motor Show. By 1956, the Firebomb had mutated into the Dual-Ghia, which now sported a set of fashionable fins. The Dual-Ghia was produced in very limited numbers between 1956 and 1963 and was powered by a Red Ram Hemi V8. Many shrewd

The last Firearrow was a four-seat convertible version of the coupe. Except for an egg-crate grille, the front end was shared with the coupe. A bold black-and-white diamond pattern leather interior overwhelmed the inside of the otherwise tastefully executed roadster. The car was sold at auction in January 2007 for $1,100,000, along with the Firearrow II.

Inset: The Ghia badge that sits on many Chrysler 'idea cars'. This is from the Firearrow IV. Main image: Dodge Firebomb. There may have been only four Firearrow 'idea cars', but the design idea developed into the little known Dodge Firebomb of 1954. Based on the sheet metal of the Firearrow IV roadster, the four-passenger Firebomb had a modified grille and utilized more traditional bumpers. The car is important in that it was the basis for the limited production Dual-Ghia. (Ford Archives UK)

buyers spent an extra $100 and went for Dodge's D-500 power option, giving an impressive 260bhp. The bodies were made in Turin and shipped to Casaroll's factory at 9760 Van Dyke, Detroit, where they were mounted to the specially prepared Dodge chassis. The elite of American society bought the new car, and as one journalist wrote: "A Rolls-Royce is a Hollywood status symbol for those who can't get a Dual-Ghia." In 1960, the Dual-Ghia received an update with the introduction of the fastback L6.4. By this time, Casaroll had sold the manufacturing rights to Ghia. Farago had already designed a high-finned model to replace the first Dual-Ghias, but found out that it looked very similar to a proposed future Chrysler production car, so he asked his friend, Ex, to redesign it. This was an important moment for Exner, as it would mean a new direction for the designer. Working at home in his free time, by the end of 1959 he had created a sleek, finless coupe with a horizontal rear end and taillight treatment that would develop into his own 1962 S series. Ex gave Farago and Segre several drawings and

sketches, which the Italians turned into reality. Twenty-six cars were built along with one prototype before the partnership between Segre and Farago became too stressful for both parties.

Returning to 1953, whilst Exner's and Segre's friendship grew stronger, Boano and Segre were coming to an impasse. Boano wanted to concentrate on the home market, whilst Segre saw the future of Ghia as a worldwide venture. In 1953, Boano sold Ghia to Segre and left to work for Fiat. Segre realized he needed another designer, one that shared his goals, so in 1954 he hired the talented Giovanni Savonuzzi away from Cisitalia to become Direttore Tecnico for Ghia. Savonuzzi was a fully qualified aerodynamicist as well as an extraordinary stylist and engineer, and was responsible for the Cisitalia D-46 and 202 coupe. As Exner had been inspired by both of these cars, the news of Savonuzzi's hiring was greeted with enthusiasm, if tainted slightly by the break-up of the relationship Ex shared with Boano.

In keeping with his stance on 'Buck Rogers' concept

1953 De Soto Adventurer in Turin, Italy.

Undoubtedly one of Virgil's favorite designs was the 1953 De Soto Adventurer, the first idea car to wear the De Soto badge. Four adults could squeeze inside this racy two-door sport coupe, which featured a host of racing styling cues, from the exposed dual lake-pipes, racing-type fuel filler cap and large racing-style gauges, to the knock-off wire wheels. The car had no trunk, just a large stowage compartment for the spare wheel.

cars, Exner's 'idea cars' were usually based on a standard New Yorker 125.5in wheelbase chassis and powered by the 331in³ Hemi V8. They were equipped with either the new PowerFlite two-speed automatic, or the older Fluid Torque transmission, depending upon when they were built. Almost all of these vehicles were drivable, sagacious automobiles, advanced enough to excite the public, but practical enough to be producible, thus expressing his belief that, "The big responsibility of the automobile stylist is not to predict what the automobile will look like many years from now, but to solve the more exacting problems of the model for next year." Another one of the cars that started in Ex's studio at home and became one of his favorite designs was the 1953 De Soto Adventurer.

After its tour of the show circuit, Ex used the Adventurer extensively, racing it at various locations around the country. It was popular with other members of the family, too. This picture of Ex and the car was taken in April 1954 at Chrysler's Chelsea proving grounds.

In 1953, Ex designed his dream car, a street roadster to replace his Studebaker Indy racer. Huge, open wire wheels and sculpted styling epitomised his feel for true automotive character, but time constraints meant that the idea only got as far as this ⅜-scale clay model.

The European looks of the two-door sport coupe gave it simple elegant lines and was the first idea car to wear the De Soto badge. Painted in cream, the car featured bucket seats for four, external exhaust pipes, recessed front grille and bumper and Exner's tell-tale radiused wheelarches and wire wheels. The car also used De Soto's own 276.1in³ Firedome Hemi V8, mated to a Fluid-Torque gearbox. It was a compact package sitting on a short 111in chassis and measuring only 189.8 inches in length, making it by far the smallest idea car to date to come from the Ghia and Exner partnership. Once the car had finished its public duties on the motor show circuit, Ex was allowed to take the car home, keeping it as his personal transportation until 1956. At some point in 1954, he had it repainted silver in the Chrysler paint shop and fitted a set of racing lights to the front. The car got noticed wherever he went. Marie Exner recalls that one night they were driving along Woodward Avenue in Detroit when they were pulled over by a police cruiser. Thinking he was in trouble, Ex stopped the car and wound the window down. To his amazement, one of the police officers asked what the car was and did he want to race to the next set of lights! Needing very little encouragement, Ex agreed and when the lights changed to green, the Hemi engine kicked in and they left the cop car in their wake. He waited at the next set of lights for the cruiser to catch up. The two police officers thanked him and turned off, impressed, if a little deflated. In 1954, Chrysler released the De Soto Adventurer II. Looked upon now as one of the most

beautiful 'idea cars' to come from the design partnership of Ghia and Exner, the Adventurer II is attributed mainly to Luigi Segre and Giovanni Savonuzzi and not the Advance Design Studio. Looking at the similarities between this car and the 1953 Cadillac Ghia which was also designed by Savonuzzi, it is easy to understand the line of thought, but it did have some typical Exner styling cues including an electrically controlled sliding rear window, wire wheels and matching luggage. The two-door sport coupe made a series of automobile salon appearances where it was the center of attention before being purchased from Chrysler by the King of Morocco in 1956. Now that Ex had his own office and modeler, he took advantage of the opportunity and designed his dream version of a street roadster. While it incorporated his fondness for the racing Ferrari grille, it mainly embodied a very narrow form, made possible by the staggered seating similar to his old Studebaker Indy racer. The long hood, massive open wire wheels and sculpted body epitomised his feeling for true automotive character. Ex fully intended to commission Ghia to build the car as a replacement for his Indy racer, so he and his personal modeler at that time, Len Klemek, built a detailed ⅜-scale clay model in his back room at Chrysler. Due to ever-increasing pressures of work, Ex never got the time to take the project any further, although some of the styling was used on the XNR 500 years later.

From this period, it is probably the 1953 Chrysler D'Elegance that is best remembered; it was the last Chrysler Ghia design to come from Ex's home studio,

Arguably the most stylish Chrysler Ghia to come from this period was the 1953 D'Elegance. A three-passenger sport coupe based on a shortened New Yorker chassis, it featured several driver conveniences, including a set of matching hand luggage accessed via the forward-folding seats. The revised gun-sight or microphone taillights would feature on future Imperials.

Photographed in Ex's home studio on Westwood Avenue, Birmingham, is the clay model for the D'Elegance. The unmistakeable silhouette would become known to thousands as the Karmann Ghia.

This front three-quarter view of the clay model shows how close the finished idea car was to the initial designs.

and in many respects the ultimate development of the K-310. Measuring considerably longer than the Adventurer (204.5in in total), the D'Elegance was a three-passenger sport coupe that featured several driver conveniences. They included a set of four luggage cases that fitted perfectly into the carpeted area behind the seats, which were covered in the same black and yellow hand-sewn leather used for the seats and door panels; a neat fold-up center armrest in the bench seat and a unique electro-hydraulic tilting spare tire mounting mechanism. Painted bright metallic coral red and wearing modified microphone taillights and a spare wheel cover on the trunk, this car would eventually become the 1956 VW Karmann Ghia.

In 1952, Volkswagen had approached Ghia, asking it to create a coupe body to fit around the Beetle chassis. Paul Farago, who had been translating for the Italians, was now directly employed by Ghia as its representative in the USA. He recalls that on a trip to Turin of that year, he saw the drawings done by Boano before he left the company. They were almost a direct copy of the car

The interior of the D'Elegance was simple but stylish. The color-coded steering wheel and instrument panel matched the cream exterior body and complemented the black and cream leather upholstery. The PowerFlite automatic gear selector can clearly be seen to the left of the steering column.

The unmistakeable silhouette of the D'Elegance, as used by Mario Boano on the VW Karmann Ghia. Ex received the first Karmann Ghia to be brought into Michigan, as a gift from Ghia. Ex passed on the car to his son.

Ghia had just finished for Chrysler, the D'Elegance. The Volkswagen had been scaled down and due to the rear engine configuration, sported a modified front end minus the grille, but it was undoubtedly the same car. It is understandable why so many would want to claim responsibility for such a classic design. Segre, Boano and Giovanni Savonuzzi all claim they designed the Karmann Ghia. Boano denied the accusation that he had stolen the essence of the Exner car, and Ex was not angered by the unauthorized plagiarism anyway. When he finally saw the production car in 1955, he was pleased with the outcome and glad

The D'Elegance had a unique electro-hydraulic mechanism for discharging the spare wheel from its recess in the trunk area. At the flick of a switch, the wheel cover popped open and the wheel was majestically pulled up and rearward for easy access. (Ford Archive UK)

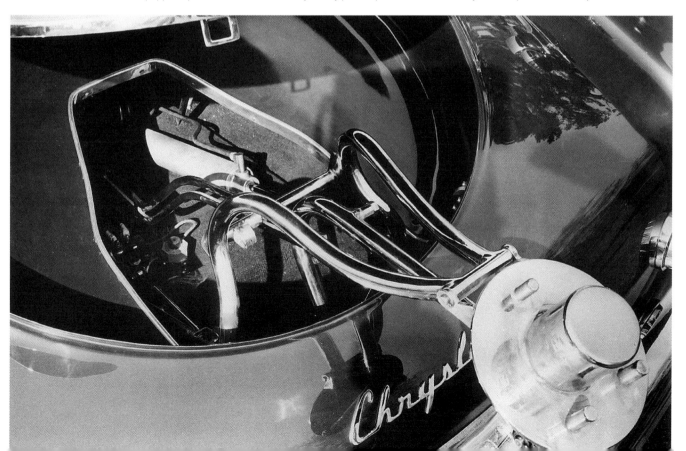

The Firearrow II from 1954 was designed by the Advanced Styling Studio in Detroit. Bodywork went almost unchanged from Mario Boano's Firearrow I design except that single headlights now appeared, molded into the fenders, and a restyled grille that was similar to the 1953 Plymouth production cars. The roadster was finished in a pale primrose color and this time around, was fully engineered with power coming from a 241.3ci Dodge Hemi V8. The car is still in pristine condition and recently sold at auction for $1,100,000. (Ford Archive UK)

The Firearrow II had two trunks; the rearmost opening held the spare wire wheel, tire, jack, and fuel filler cap, while just behind the cockpit was another trunk for personal belongings. Both of these storage areas had electrically operated opening devices.

The aircraft-like cockpit was a study in simple splendor. A black leather bench seat overlooked the sporty wooden rimmed steering wheel and the two large nacelles that held the all important gauges. As with the first Firearrow, the windshield was a raked-back, one-piece, unframed screen made of strengthened glass. Being a true roadster, the cockpit remained open to the elements as no canopy or side windows were provided for the car.

that one of his designs had made it into large-scale production. Between 1955 and 1974, some 360,000 coupes and 80,000 cabriolets were built at the Karmann plant in Osnabruck, Germany, making this the most accessible Exner-Ghia designed car ever. Virgil Exner Jr claims that he owned the first ever Karmann Ghia to arrive in the state of Michigan. In 1952, Ghia also built a Ferrari sport coupe for the Paris Salon based very much on the lines of Exner's Chrysler SS cars, and again in 1953, it built a Fiat 1100 Abarth sport coupe for the Turin show that was heavily inspired by Exner's styling.

The fast pace of creating ideas continued in the Advance Styling Studio. A Crown Imperial Limousine was styled and again built by Ghia. The studio also took Boano's Firearrow and developed it further for the Firearrow II, III and IV, all built in 1954. The collaboration between Ex and the Italian designers was inspirational. Seeing the smooth lines of European coupes and the finned aerodynamic racing cars in vogue on the continent, led Ex to investigate a more flowing, dart-like approach to his proposals. His sketches at home were starting to show

the first tentative buds of metallic fins, but the workload at the studio was just about to increase even further, forcing him to put these embryonic ideas to one side for a while.

Keller's protégé and heir to the presidential throne, Lester Lum (Tex) Colbert became Chrysler President on the 3rd November 1950, when K T Keller was 'retired' upstairs to the position of Chairman of the Board. Keller still had a tight rein on production styling and as late as 1951, he was still vetoing the use of gimmicks like curved front windscreens, which he finally allowed for the 1953 model year. Chrysler Corporation was in dire straits, both Colbert and Keller had been impressed by Exner's concepts, but the production vehicles were not selling. Virgil Exner Jr claims that Keller showed his father plans for the 'make or break' 1955 models in the fall of 1952, asking his opinion. Ex answered in one word: "Lousy". The stylist shook his head and told the chairman that the cars would be a sales disaster. Keller offered Exner the opportunity of redesigning the entire '55 range, but with production due to start in July 1954, giving only eighteen months to achieve this monumental task, this was a major

This publicity shot taken from a 1953 Chrysler brochure emphasized styling throughout, with the men who were the driving force. Left to right, James C Zeder, Vice President of Engineering, Virgil Exner, Director of Styling, and Tex Colbert, President.

Ex reorganized the styling department and, for the first time in Chrysler's history, took control of the clay rooms. This was where the stylist's creations were realized in three dimensions. The popular designs achieved full-size clay models, as with the one seen here.

The Imperial became a separate marque in 1955 and carried many of the Exner styling cues seen on the K-310. Radiused wheelarches, machine gun-sight taillights and single-tone paintwork emphasised the classy look of Chrysler's top line offering.

undertaking. Another caveat was that he would have to utilize the frames used for the '54s. Exner agreed on the understanding that the modelers needed would answer to him and not the engineers, as had previously been the case. Cliff Voss recalled, "Ex changed the way cars were styled at Chrysler. Originally K T would pick the renderings, and the body engineers, headed by U L Thomas, would lay out the body draft based on the rendering. The draftsmen would follow the clays – not the stylists. The stylists weren't allowed in the clay rooms!" It is interesting to note that at this time, all of the 'idea cars' coming from the advanced design studio were accredited to Chrysler Engineering Division and not to styling. Engineers still ruled the roost and up to that time the production car bodies had been designed by Charlie Walker in the engineering drafting room. Dick Burke, another stylist employed by Exner agrees, "Walker and Keller would go into the drafting room and slam the door closed and work out the bodies. Then the designers would get a look at it and add moldings here and there, that's all they did. Until Ex took over, the whole place was run by engineers for engineers." It must have been a hard pill to swallow, but K T approved Ex's request and work began.

Initial drawings were predictably based on the K-310 but Ex struggled to make the design fit well to a four-door sedan body. One design got as far as a full-size wooden

1955 De Soto. Sharing similar lines to the Chrysler, the De Soto shrugged off its dowdy, bank manager reputation in 1955 to reveal a stylish and powerful mode of transport. This would be the last year for the toothy De Soto grille.

mock-up, which was displayed in engineering's sixth-floor showroom. According to Cliff Voss the car was maroon and black and very chic, but when it came to whether it should become a production vehicle, he and Exner agreed that it was too futuristic and they didn't want another Airflow on their hands. Ex, Voss and Harry Chesebrough (head of Engineering Product Planning) called a meeting. Voss remembered: "With those 'blister' K-310 front fenders, the bodyside proved hard to ornament, especially in the various iterations required for three car lines. I somewhat timorously suggested adapting the parade car sides to the '55's. Exner and Harry laughed; they had already decided to do just that. We kept the roof of Exner's car and used the parade car design below

the belt." The Imperial was created first and was the car that carried the most styling cues from the K-310. Fully exposed wheelarches showed off the luxury wire wheels, the stylised eagle ornament on the hood, and of course the machine gun rear taillights. When the 1955 Imperial launched (as a separate marque from 1955), it exuded style, finesse and luxury.

The Imperial was followed by Chrysler, then De Soto. They shared similar lines and gently curved wheelarches, but the De Soto wore a more ornate grille that would see the last use of the familiar toothy grille. More importantly, the Chrysler wore chrome rear light-bezels that sat on top of the rear fenders, forming small but not insignificant fins. This, then, was how Ex would test the waters for

the 'Forward Look' logo and slogan, both of which had been dreamed up by New York advertising company McCann-Erickson. The cars were a huge success in what was a boom year generally. Sales jumped from 883,769 in 1954 up to 1,579,215 for '55, almost giving Chrysler its target market share of 20 per cent in one fell swoop as it reached 16.8 per cent.

By October 1953, long before the debut of the 1955 models, Tex Colbert could see where Ex was going with his designs, and on the basis of this and the success of the 'idea cars', Exner became Chrysler's first Director of Styling, aged just 44. Occupying a position created specifically for him, and more important than the name itself, the promotion meant that finally, Ex could get involved with the production cars. He took control of the small styling department, working with King, and immediately started to make changes. At that time, styling was divided into six separate studios: Henry King controlled Plymouth, Herb Weissinger covered Dodge, Plymouth was under Tom Bannister, and Chrysler was managed by Tom Martin. Ex's Advanced Studio and a separate Truck and Special Projects Studio made up the numbers. Between them, Exner and King brought the studios together and started a recruitment campaign that brought in some very talented people like Bill Brownlie, Bill Robinson, Jack Kennets and Don Kopka, many of them coming from Chrysler's recent acquisition of Briggs Manufacturing Company. Exner's dislike of paperwork and administration grew in relation to his workload, so, in October of 1954, he hired Carl Reynolds, who he knew from his time at Pontiac to be his styling administrator. By spring 1956, the styling staff numbered nearly 300 strong. While work continued with the designs for 1955, in what little time was available, Ex did what he could to spruce up the already completed 1954 models with most of his time spent on the Dodge cars.

A car worthy of special note here is the 1954

reaction to his planned introduction of a new finned car. Dodge and Plymouth were completely restyled too, and shared some sheet metal between them. Styled by Maury Baldwin and Henry King, they were longer, lower, wider; the small Plymouth was gone, replaced by a striking vehicle that The Society of Illustrators voted 'The Most Beautiful Car Of The Year'. So different were these vehicles, the assembly line at the Lynch Road Plant had to be extended 27ft to facilitate production. Color usage for all of the divisions was an important part of the styling package. Body inserts called 'color sweeps' were used extensively to allow for more color combinations. Some 56 solid colors were made available, with 173 two or three-tone options listed. When they were launched at the press meeting on the 17th November 1954, the complete line-up was advertised as 'The 100 Million Dollar Look' in deference to the cost of development and retooling. By May of 1955, all corporation cars were using

Plymouth Belmont. While General Motors was developing the Corvette, one of the engineers working on the Corvette project talked to Al Prance at Briggs Manufacturing about the new two-seater sportscar that was being made of fiberglass. K T Keller got to hear about it and authorised Prance to start secretly working on an alternative design for Chrysler using the same production methods and similar dimensions, with the styling created by Bill Robinson. A major stipulation was that Robinson had to use stock parts wherever possible, including bumpers and light bezels. Just as work on the car was nearing completion, Chrysler bought Briggs and the Belmont became an official Chrysler design. The Belmont was largely a 1954 Dodge, utilising the chassis and running gear from Dodge's own 114in wheelbase convertible and two-door cars. The dream car was, however, fitted with Plymouth's Hy-Drive semi-automatic transmission mated to a Dodge 241.3in^3 V8. Standing just 49in tall, the deliciously low-slung convertible was

originally painted in a light silvery blue. The car had a very aerodynamic theme, from its aircraft-type cockpit to the fuselage body styling that was very avant-garde for the time. So as not to spoil the smooth lines of the car, the soft-top cover folded away in a hidden compartment behind the seats. Released in a year when Plymouth was struggling to sell anything at all, Plymouth dealers wanted the Belmont put into immediate production, but Chrysler bosses disagreed; they thought the car looked too dated and dropped the concept. Sales continued to fall. Robinson remembers that shortly after its release, Ex walked into the Plymouth Studio where he was by then working, "Ex came up to me and said, 'Bill, would you mind if I took the credit for the Plymouth Belmont?' He was really nice about it, and I replied, 'Man, you can have credit for that thing if you want it' because for years I wouldn't even admit that I was responsible for it but now I guess it stood the test of time and I feel proud of it." Plymouth dealers did not give up that easily; they had

In October 1953, Ex became Chrysler Corporation's first Director of Styling, a post created especially for him.

It's only human to get a glow when others view your car with admiring eyes.
The satisfaction of Plymouth owners doesn't end here. For they know
that their car contains admirable traits you can't see in a glance—
advanced engineering, quality materials, honest craftsmanship, and an enduring
performance that constantly sustains their judgment in choosing a Plymouth.

PLYMOUTH

Chrysler Corporation's No. 1 Car

The Plymouth Cranbrook Convertible Club Coupe, shown at the Shadow Mountain Club, Palm Desert, near Palm Springs, Calif.

Plymouth Studio 1954. At the back table sits Plymouth Studio Manager Hal Pilkey, the man responsible for the quad headlamp cowls on later 1958 cars. In front of him is Charles 'Bud' Gitschlag, while Ex talks to stylist Dave Scott. The windows to the right faced east towards the Engineering buildings and windows out of view on the left faced west onto Oakland Ave in Highland Park. The building they were in was called the Styling building and concentrated mostly on exterior design. The interiors were done in another area.

The Plymouth Belmont was designed by Bill Robinson before he came from Briggs Manufacturing to Chrysler. Built in fiberglass and originally finished in light metallic blue, this lovely low-slung sportscar featured minimal ornamentation and white leather bucket seats. A center console held the radio and power antenna controls. The car has now been painted red and is a common sight at car shows throughout America.

heard rumors that Dodge and De Soto were going to get a performance car for the 1956 model year and knew that they could move a great many Plymouth hot cars. Their persistence paid off when a special project coded FA, presumably after the Firearrow, eventually became the Fury project.

Of the all-new 1955 Chrysler range, undoubtedly the limited production Chrysler C-300 was the most significant release. Although the new range from Chrysler Corporation offered a great deal to the drivers of America, three influential men at Chrysler recognized that there was still a gap in the line-up. Chief Engineer of Chrysler Division Robert M Rodger, Sales Manager Ed Braden and Virgil Exner all agreed that what was needed to make the most of Chrysler's record-breaking Hemi engine was a production sportscar. Unfortunately, the corporation was not in a financial situation where it could afford to create a car to match the Corvette or the up-and-coming

Thunderbird. What it could do was make a factory hot rod; a lighter car fitted with the largest engine available, much like Buick's Century models. By late 1954, the team had created a viable prototype performance car using the body of a Chrysler Windsor but with the front grille from the new Imperial, accentuated by simple understated chrome detailing. This unique car used parts that were all stock items, from the 300bhp Hemi engine and New Yorker instrument panel, to the heavy-duty Imperial running gear. Cliff Voss orchestrated the minimalist style and created the unique checkered flag badge that sat between the split grille. Chrysler executives gave the go-ahead and on 17th January 1955 publicly announced the release of the new car. On 10th February, the first C-300 rolled off the Imperial assembly line at the Jefferson Avenue plant; a vehicle that would begin a series of sports touring cars that would become legendary.

It was at this time that Ex created a car for himself,

a car that embodied everything that he wanted to see in a classic automobile; sports thoroughbred styling and power to match. Exner rarely came up with the names given to his 'idea cars' at Chrysler, but one he did select was the Falcon from 1955. He wanted Chrysler to build a vehicle that could compete against Chevrolet's Corvette and Ford's Thunderbird. Largely forgotten now, the A488 Falcon was a joint effort between Maury Baldwin and Ex, getting valuable input from some quarters of the engineering staff. As with their previous endeavours, they sent a small model and plans

The October 1954 issue of Car Life *magazine featured Virgil Exner and some of his 'idea cars'. In the six pages dedicated to him, Ex set out his stall, explaining his beliefs on where car styling should be going.*

for the car over to Turin. Luigi Segre used his considerable engineering talent to transform the design into a real car. Not a dream car or even an idea car, but a prototype that was a breath away from becoming a production vehicle. The Falcon was a two-seat sportscar that sat on a short 109in Chrysler chassis and although not revolutionary, was perfect for its time. Delicious smooth surfaces and minimal chrome work accentuated Exner's styling cues. The long, low hood covered a Hemi V8 and standard Chrysler mechanics, and perched on top of an aggressive front grille and recessed headlamp pods. The low silhouette of just 51.2in added to the perception of speed and power, the flowing lines ending in subtle tail fins that finished over jet-like taillight bezels. Fully open wheelarches displayed Kelsey-Hayes wire wheels and wide white-wall tires. Sporty exterior exhaust pipes exited from the rocker panels and complemented the side louvers on the front fenders. Because Ex was hoping the car would go into production, many parts were taken from the Chrysler 'parts bin', including suspension, steering, and brake system components, making the project more attractive to executives. This was not a small car, at 182in it was longer than both of its potential competitors, but would undoubtedly have stolen some of their custom.

Three identical bodies were built in 1955, colored metallic red, metallic blue and raven black. The reason it did not go into production was down to the engineering department's wish for control over style. Its argument was that it had performance vehicles in the up-and-coming 1956 line, with the Chrysler 300B, Dodge D-500, and the rest. Why build a sportscar? Bill Brownlie, a studio manager who worked for Ex through this period, states it was more fundamental than that: "My remembrance of the head of engineering, the power at that time, was that he liked Exner, but I think also the same person who held him back was Paul Ackerman. [He was] a great engineer, of course, but he didn't know anything about styling. He didn't know anything about product, but again, because of engineering's dominance ... I think they used [their power] wrongly when it came to trying to develop new products, and I think they were always hesitant in that they didn't want to cave in to Ex and his desires. I think what they wanted to do is say, 'Well, Ex, now you design these cars but we'll tell you how to engineer them.' Well, when they did that, they destroyed the very essence of what Ex was trying to develop, in my opinion, and it held him back as a result of that, and that really hurt the company, too."

Two more 'idea cars' were built for 1955 and were more prophetic in styling. The Flight Sweep I convertible and its hard-top sister, Flight Sweep II, were based on 1954 De Soto chassis and running gear, and fitted

1955 Chrysler C-300. All of the Forward Look cars were stunning, but none more so than Chrysler's new factory hot rod, the C-300. Introduced later than the other models, on 17th January 1955, the simply executed design was based on a Chrysler Windsor two-door coupe, but with the addition of an Imperial grille and minimal ornamentation. The heart of the car was a 300bhp, 331.1ci Hemi V8.

with the 276in³ V8. They shared the same body panels and, this time around, the 'trashcan lid' spare wheel cover on the trunk did actually cover the spare, which was mounted on a second deck. The larger fins and eager stance of the pair, along with the Falcon, foretold what was around the corner. When they went on show throughout America, Chrysler stated that these cars "carried the spirit of the Forward Look". In an article for *Road & Track* dated November 1955, Exner stated that

It all started here, Chrysler's first fin on a production car. The 1955 Chryslers all wore this new style, formed by the chrome light bezel, looking its best on the rear of a C-300.

"in the modern jet fighter plane the nose is tapered and the bulk seems concentrated toward the rear, crowned by the upsweep of the tail. Big racing boats take the same general form, which is even accentuated by the rooster tail of water thrown up behind them at high speed. The wedge-like silhouette is also apparent in powerful racing cars. Our styling of the 'idea cars' was based on these impressions because we found them both valid and pleasing to the eye. In Flight Sweep I and Flight Sweep II the rear fenders and taillights were swept up into a fin. A color line begins with the fin and extends forward and gradually upward, ending in front fender extensions that carry beyond the headlights and seem to lead the car ahead. These same techniques are apparent to a lesser degree in the Falcon in which the mechanical aspects are emphasized in keeping with its likeness to modern competition sportscars." Exner replaced his much-loved Adventurer with the black Falcon, and just as he had done with the previous show

Ex behind the wheel of his Falcon at the start line of a time trial racing event.

1955 Flight Sweep I. The Flight Sweep I and its hard-top sister were quite prophetic in their styling. The higher fins were how Exner saw the near future of automobile design.

car, he often took the car to meetings and gatherings of the Sportscar Club of America, of which he was still an enthusiastic member, putting the car through its paces to the delight of fellow members and visitors.

The styling studios worked hard on the face-lifts for 1956 and 1957, as well as an evolutionary all-new design for 1958. To accommodate the growing needs of the styling section, in 1956, the whole department moved from engineering to purpose-built offices in Building 128 on the northern edge of the Highland Park complex. With Ex's guidance, the Studios and the previously separated clay rooms were finally integrated. Ex moved into a separate studio of his own, accompanied only by clay modeler George Motorojescu. He actually had two offices – a large office that he used for visitors and a smaller office with a secret studio built in the back. It was here that he spent most of his time.

Exner had worked hard on the 1955 models but, not wanting to rest on his laurels, he toiled even harder on the face-lift '56 cars. With a very limited tooling budget, he managed to create even more exciting cars, mainly through the addition of small but significant fins. By changing just the rear quarter-panels and sedan rear doors the new cars took on a new look; a forward look. Each design was unique but with distinct family ties to

Here Exner explains the styling advances of the Flight Sweep I show car to a group of Chrysler dealers. Ex attended many seminars as guest speaker.

Clockwise from top left: 1955 Plymouth Plainsman. Not many would argue that this station wagon lacked style or taste. It did have many features that would later be seen on production models, such as power-operated roll-down rear windows, rear-facing back seats and spare wheel mounted in the right rear fender. The federal tax laws required that any concept cars that were brought into the country to be used for show purposes did not have to pay an import duty if they were sent out of the country within fourteen months. This particular car was sent to Cuba and given to the president of the Cuban banks. After he was assassinated, Chrysler gave the car to the international export manager for Chrysler who lived in Cuba. He escaped with the car during Castro's coup and returned to the United States. Thereafter he was sent by Chrysler to Australia and, of course, took his favorite car with him, the 1955 Chrysler Ghia station wagon. After many years in Australia, he returned to the United States and eventually the car ended up in a private collection. (Ford Archive UK); Plainsman Interior. The electrically-powered seats, which were upholstered in brown and white unborn calfskin, could be lowered to make a huge double bed in the cargo area. Thankfully, this idea was dropped! The exterior of the car was painted palomino beige metallic. (Ford Archive UK); Exner joins a discussion with engineer Paul Ackermann and former head stylist Henry King in 1955. Although Ex got on well with Ackerman on a personal level, the engineer resented losing control of design to the stylist.

The 1955 Ghia Gilda, although not strictly an Exner car, was strongly inspired by his styling cues, and ultimately, the Gilda would inspire Exner. The un-powered Gilda was designed by Giovanni Savonuzzi using the wind tunnel at the Turin Polytechnic and was created by watching ink blots being blown into a dart shape. First introduced on the Ghia stand at the 1955 Turin Motor Show, the car mutated several times over the next five years, still being shown in 1960.

the 1955 and 1956 models, Ex formulated and honed his ideas for the 1958 models. Occasionally he would take a team of designers out to Indianapolis as a treat, meeting up with his racing friends. Speaking recently to some of his ex-colleagues, they all agreed that when Ex spoke to

each other. Plymouth received the most aeronautical styling with its tall, thin fins and jet-like exhausts, while Dodge introduced a kicked-back fin above twin tower taillights. De Soto fins were more graceful and reached their peak above what would become a fifties icon, the triple tower rocketship taillights. Chrysler and Imperial models, quite correctly, had the most elegant fins of all. The overall impression was one of motion. At the time of their release, Exner said, "We wanted to give the Forward Look cars an appearance of fleetness, the eager, poised for action look, which we feel is the natural and functional shape of automobiles." Except for the Imperial, this year saw the introduction of performance versions of all marques, to join the already successful Chrysler 300 from 1955. The Chrysler 300B was joined by De Soto's release of the Adventurer, Dodge had the D-500 model, and Plymouth offered the Fury. All of them were superb performance cars which, along with the fresh new styling, helped Chrysler to shed its dowdy, conservative image. Through the success of

1956 Chrysler tail. The stylish simplicity of the 1956 Chryslers makes it as pleasing to look at today as when first introduced.

1956 Dodge D-500. Not just another package, the D-500 was a model in its own right, alongside De Soto's Adventurer, the Chrysler 300B and the Plymouth Fury. This record-breaking model was Dodge's first muscle car, but unfortunately, owing to dealers offering a D-500 package mid-season on any Dodge, it watered down the model's exclusivity and is now all but forgotten. This is probably the rarest, the D-500 Golden Royal Lancer, thought to be the only surviving example built for the Californian market.

you it was as a fellow stylist not as a vice president of the third largest automobile manufacturer in North America – he was honest, quietly spoken, and down to earth. One of those colleagues Bill Robinson explained how the stylists planned the proposals to the vice presidents: "One thing we learned is that making a presentation to the divisions, you don't present to them six different cars because you don't get a majority and no one is happy. Internally, we would make some decisions; we would get all of the designers together, all of the engineers and clay modelers and some other

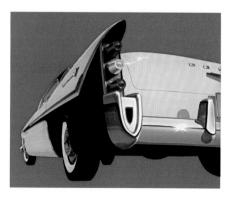

1956 De Soto. The triple taillights, first seen in 1956, were designed by Jack Kennets, and would become a '50s icon.

people and get a miniature consensus. Then what we would do was present just two models, one of them would be the one you hoped the VPs would pick and the other was a real dog. This way you got a majority".

It was at this time that Exner helped to put together one of the most important and lucrative contracts Ghia would receive from Chrysler. The plan was to create a very limited production run of luxury limousines based on an Imperial platform, in order to challenge Cadillac and Lincoln. The initial order was for twenty-five Imperials for delivery between November 1956 and May 1957, with the first one going on sale on 2nd January 1957. Designed by Exner with help from Bill Brownlie and Cliff Voss, the standard 129in wheelbase Imperial convertible chassis were shipped from the United States by sea, with an unfinished two-door hard-top body, minus doors, windows or seats. The components were shipped separately: windows, doors, air conditioning plant, and even the paint. At Ghia, they cut the car, removed the roof completely, and stretched the X-member chassis to a wheelbase of 149.5in, adding custom-formed base, roof

Virgil, Henry King, the manager of the Plymouth Studio, and Bud Gitschlag (seated) in the Plymouth Studio in late 1955, discuss the merits of the Plymouth front grille on Bill Robinson's design for 1957.

and side panels as required, along with 1958 style grilles and trim. Doors were modified so that they extended into the roof, meaning special roof panels had to be created to match. Extensive mechanical alterations included adding a longer propeller shaft, and fuel, brake, and exhaust lines. Each car was then finished by hand, using up to 150lb of lead filling, before being painted in several layers of either black, dark blue, dark green or maroon lacquer, and then shipped back to America, where they sold for approximately $12,000. It is thought that thirty-six cars were built in this style, with yearly updates until the contract ceased in 1965. The 132 Crown Imperials (not

This sketch was done by Dave Cummins from the Imperial Studio in October 1956, and although outlandish, would provide inspiration for a Ghia-built prototype car in 1959, based on the Plymouth 250 Valiant.

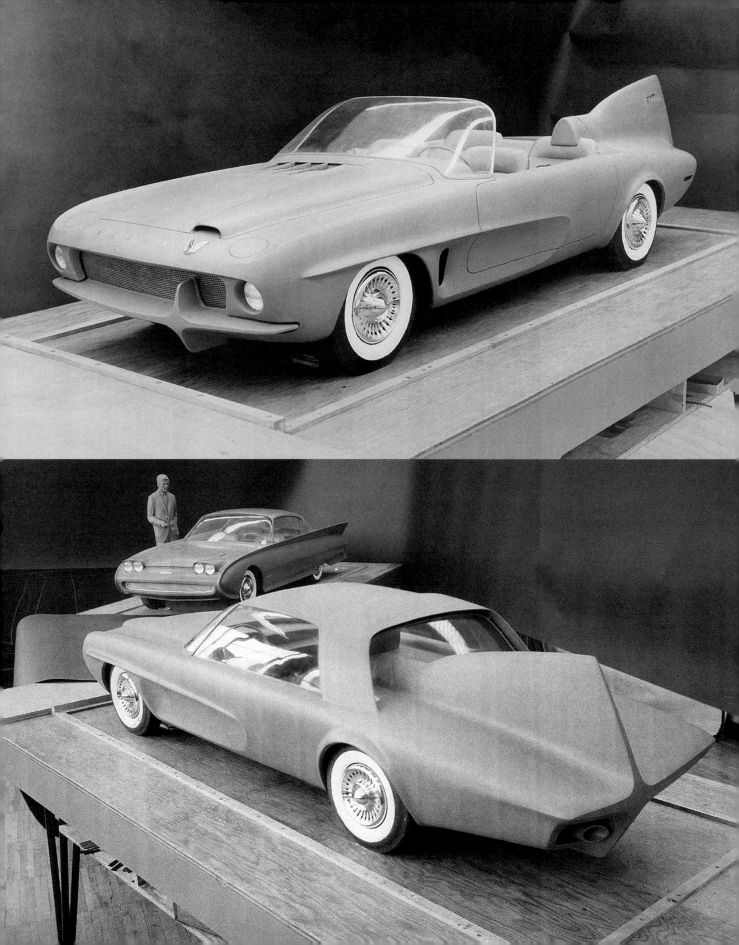

to be confused with the standard Imperial Crown series) built through that time sold for twice as much as a standard Imperial, and for a lot less than it cost to produce them, so became much sought-after by royalty, millionaire businessmen, and movie stars alike. Owners and passengers have included Jacqueline Kennedy, General MacArthur, Nelson Rockefeller, the King of Saudi Arabia, Pearl Buck, the Shah of Iran, and the Queen of England.

By far the largest car to be seen at the Turin Motor Show in January 1957 was the eight-passenger Crown Imperial Limousine Presedenziale, as it was known to Ghia, one of the first Crown Imperials to be built by Ghia in an ongoing contract that would last until 1964. Each car took four-and-a-half weeks to produce, with almost half of that time spent on paint and trim. The interior was trimmed in high quality broadcloth, the finest supple leather, and fine woods. Carpeting for passengers was luxurious sheared mouton, while the driver's area and trunk space used hard-wearing black nylon carpeting. The vinyl-covered landau roof gave a very formal look and helped to hide a large amount of lead filler.

Exner continued his quest to create a car with optimal all-round visibility. His most daring step in this direction was the ill-fated Norseman. Ex got the initial idea from one of his advanced engineers and worked closely with Bill Brownlie, Cliff Voss, and Chrysler engineers for over two years to create a design that was in many ways very unconventional, but at the same time adopting a style that had not been popular since the late 1940s. The car sported two cantilevered steel arches curving upward and forward from the frame at the rear. There were no pillars or supports, not even at the outer extremities of the wraparound windshield. Fine ⅝in steel rods each side of the windshield tied the roof down, offering unparalleled vision except to the rear. Lightweight aluminum body-panels offset the large beam weight used to give the car its structural strength. The idea was that if the car rolled over, the thin rods at the front would snap

1957 Crown Imperial Convertible. This Ghia-built Imperial is reportedly the world's longest convertible and was built for Sarabdullah Mubarak Alsabak, the Sultan of Kuwait in 1957. (Ford Archive UK)

and the cantilever roof would spring up and act as a rollover bar, lessening injury. Other innovations included a 12ft^2 power-operated rear windscreen that slid upward into the roof and a full-length belly pan under the body to aid aerodynamic efficiency. The use of a fastback or sloping rear deck was an unusual choice to lay-people but, from an engineering standpoint, it gave the Norseman its greatest chance of success. The two-door coupe seated four in comfortable metallic green and grey leather bucket seats that matched the metallic green body paint. Unique reel-type seat belts were mounted in the doors and special air-intakes for the cockpit were built into the leading edge of the roof panel. The sleek exterior was accentuated by the hidden headlamps and lack of door handles. Voss and Ex travelled to Ghia with the plans for the car. The Norseman was named because of Exner's ancestry and would become the most expensive experimental car to be built by Chrysler thus far. It was a testament to Sergio Coggiola, head of Ghia's prototype workshop, and Segre's engineering skills that the car was completed only a few weeks over schedule, but it did miss its intended sailing. Not unduly worried, Segre booked the

One of the most adventurous 'idea cars' ever to be built was the 1956 Chrysler Norseman. Wearing a fastback roofline and streamlined underbelly, the car featured a unique cantilevered roof that was held down by two thin rods of steel on each side of the windscreen. If the car rolled, the rods were designed to snap and flip up the roof, protecting the occupants. This rare photo from Ghia shows the wooden buck used in the production of body panels in the courtyard at Ghia.

outlook was grim and his immediate family were told to expect the worst. Virgil Jr came back from where studying at the University of Notre Dame to look after his sisters Bronwen and Marie, while Mildred kept a vigil at Ex's bedside. For the next few days he was kept semi-conscious, enveloped in an oxygen tent. Slowly he regained his strength. Five days after his heart attack, Tex Colbert, Mildred and Virgil Jr sat around his bed looking worried. Having only seen

On 17th July 1956, the Norseman set sail from Genoa to New York on the Italian Liner Andrea Doria

The interior of the Norseman has rarely been seen, but this shot clearly shows the thin steel rods used to hold the roof in place, and the metallic-green bucket seats separated by a large center console. (Beaulieu Motoring Museum)

car onto the next available ship to America, the Italian liner *Andrea Doria*.

Throughout this time, Exner's health was beginning to deteriorate. Not just the energy he put into the designs for the 1957 models, but years of chain smoking, drinking gallons of coffee, an intolerance to alcohol and the constant battle with the manufacturing and engineering departments finally took their toll. On 24th July 1956, he was rushed to the William Beaumont Hospital in Birmingham after suffering a major heart attack. Almost straight away, he underwent open-heart surgery. The

blueprints and sketches, Ex asked how the latest idea car had turned out. Unsure whether they should tell him or not, Tex finally drummed up courage and broke the news that the car was at the bottom of the sea.

The *Andrea Doria* was a luxury ocean liner for the Italian Line (Società di navigazione Italia), and had a gross tonnage of 29,100 and a capacity of just over 1200 passengers and 563 crew. For a country attempting to rebuild its economy and reputation after World War II, the *Andrea Doria* was an icon of Italian national pride. Of all Italy's ships at the time, this was the largest, fastest, and supposedly safest. The liner brimmed with original modern artwork, paintings, and sculptures, and was often described as a floating gallery. In the second week of July, the Norseman was carefully crated and taken to the dockyard at Genoa. Normally, all passenger cars were placed in the garage section of the *Andrea Doria* that sat slightly aft of the bow wing bridge. These cars would have been placed onto the Doria by use of a crane

and meticulously parked in the garage and arranged strategically for stability. The Norseman, however, was no ordinary passenger vehicle and was specially packed and treated with extra care. On 17th July, as passengers began to board the luxury liner, the Norseman, still in its wooden crate, was placed in the number 2 cargo area, ready for its trip to New York. The ship departed at 11:00am on the 4000 mile journey to America, stopping in Cannes on the French Riviera, then Naples, then Gibraltar before leaving the Mediterranean and heading west into the North Atlantic Ocean. On the evening of 25th July, the last night of the journey, another liner, the SS Stockholm of the Swedish-American Line crashed into the *Andrea Doria* in thick fog, just of the coast of Nantucket, Massachusetts. The impact opened a large gash below the starboard wing bridge, causing such a gaping hole in the Doria's side that within minutes the ship was leaning dangerously to its right side, flooding watertight compartments that kept the ship afloat. It took precisely eleven hours to sink, giving ample time to evacuate 1660 people. Tragically, 51 people lost their lives, 5 from the Stockholm and the rest from the Italian liner.

When Ex heard the news, he was upset by the loss of life, but rather than be saddened by the loss of the Norseman, he gave a wry laugh. He quite correctly predicted that the car would become a part of seafaring legend and was a better end than the ignominious fate that awaited its arrival. It is thought that the complete development of this automobile cost almost $100,000 1956 dollars, but would have been a waste of money if the car did not respond how it was supposed to. The only way to find out was a controlled destruction. After the car had finished touring in 1957, it was due to be crashed at the Chelsea Proving Grounds to ascertain whether the cantilever roof worked. Far better that it should be lost at sea and become folklore. Many industry observers have questioned why the Norseman was never replicated. Virgil Jr replies: "You had to get on with things. It was a waste of time to go back and rebuild it in any way, even though there were probably hammer forms left over, and that wouldn't have taken too much effort, and Chrysler collected on the insurance, of course. But the thinking was that by the time you design anything, it's obsolete, so my father probably thought that rather than have it duplicated, let's take that money and do the newest thing that is in his mind." The radical cantilevered roof idea was never raised again by Chrysler.

Just before Exner's heart attack, he had met with old friend and racing car builder Frank Kurtis. Kurtis

---

JOHN C. GUENTHER

31 July 1956

"Hey, Luigi, wad you got there?"

"Itsa ledder from Meester Ex."

"So? Why you look so sad? Dat Ex, heesa nica guy!"

"Sure, heesa greata guy. He can keess da behind!"

"Wad you mean, Luigi? Dat Ex...he maka da trubbles?"

"He gonna sue!"

"Sue? Why he wanna sue?"

"He no lika da last car. He say she stink!"

"Stink! Shesa da bes car yet. We maka da beeg pro-duck. We give da bigga deal when da guys from Detroit come here and maka wid all da beeg wurds lika exec. Wad he mean da car stink? Lemme see da lett fromma da Ex. Where he say she stink?"

"Here. He say, 'Luigi, you giva da money back or I sue. Dat car no good. She no float....she sink.'"

FROM JOHN GUENTHER - CHRYSLER STYLING P.R. DIRECTOR (ENGINEERING)

REGARDING THE ANDREA DORIA SINKING WITH THE 'NORSEMAN' ABOARD - WHILE FATHER IN HOSPITAL AFTER 1ST HEART ATTACK.

— VME JR. 1956

LUIGI SEGRE IS OWNER OF GHIA)

This 'get well' note was given to Ex by close friend and head of Chrysler Engineering Public Relations, John Guenther. The spoof conversation is supposed to be between Paul Farago and head of Ghia, Luigi Segre.

This amusing piece was written by Virgil Exner around 1949 and gives a wonderful insight into the complexities of car design and the frustrations suffered by the designers.

Three things the average businessman can do instinctively: write a great advertisement, play an astute game of poker (when he gets the cards), and design a beautiful automobile. Although I'm in no position to second guess his advertising genius or his poker hands, I can appreciate his flair for design. Anyone with a pencil and a piece of paper can do the job.

But there is a catch in it. Experience has taught me that it's a long, tortuous road from the sketchpad to the assembly line. Manufacturing problems are a controlling factor. Driving safely must be considered. There's a problem called 'roadability' that can never be solved on the drawing board. Then, sales officials will argue plausibly that they want an automobile and not an autogyro. By and large, customers seem fond of modern car design. The public lacks the taste for Buck Rogers.

For the purpose of citing a few difficulties in sound car designing, let's say that your particular effort has been awarded a $25,000 top prize by the Blinx Motor Company and that they have promised to put it into production. Let's assume further that your brain plum carries the streamlined motif 19 years ahead of the pack (as I'm sure it would), introduces a lovely filigreed grille, a tapered tail with fins, and hugs the road like gravy on a new suit.

Your creation goes to the design department. The head designer looks it over and, after admiring your $25,000 check, offers a 'suggestion.' He says, "The first thing we establish here is the wheelbase. This isn't entirely because more wheelbase increases cost. The factory assembly line is just so long and no longer. When you add the wheelbase of your car, you reduce the capacity of the assembly line. So we'll cut the wheelbase down to what our factory considers a workable length. Okay?"

Naturally, you agree. The statement makes sense. He sends your design to the modeling department some 15 inches shorter than your original intentions.

From your plans a modeler builds a quarter-size replica of an automobile. He fashions a model of clay and casts the car in plaster. Then miniature fittings are made, paint is applied, and your design is exactly proportioned in three dimensions. To you it looks good.

About this time, a representative of the sales department drops in. A gleam comes to his eye, which you probably misinterpret. "How long is that job?" he asks. You are well armed for the query. Patiently you explain about the length of the assembly line and how the car has been designed for 'standard production'.

"I don't care about that stuff," he says. "What's the overall length? The average garage is 20 feet long. This thing will have its tail sticking out in the open all year round. Shorten it up!"

The designer backs up the sales official. He calls the modeler again and another quarter-size image is built up, somewhat shorter, not quite so effective, and yet still carrying much of your 'advanced thinking.'

No one offers any criticisms of the model before the next step. (We deviate somewhat from general practice here. If there's any point in a new-car development where the design escapes criticism, it must be that the work is being done by a crew of deaf mutes behind locked doors.)

Anyway, the modeler works up a full-size model in clay. Now is the time for your old pal, the designer, to get nasty. He circles the clay model, squinting and muttering about 'compound surfaces'. Finally, he motions you over. "See that highlight on the roof?" he asks. You do, now that he mentions it. "See how the reflections make your car look cockeyed." You smile indulgently and remark that it must be "the way the light hits it". "Exactly," he says. "But walk around the car and notice how it hangs on. Try to picture the car on a showroom floor. That highlight may be the very thing that would convince a prospect to shop next door. Nope, the roof surface will have to be changed."

You know this guy is merely suffering from an unrequited pang of professional jealousy. No one ever heard of designing a car by highlights. However, you decide to be magnanimous. The curve of the roof is flattened.

About here the chassis engineer calls. Ordinarily, he wouldn't appear in person, he'd just glance at the specifications and start screaming. Inasmuch as you have taken his and his'n (?) for 25 grand, he may be curious about what you look like. He begins courteously enough, although a quaver can be detected in his voice. "Just a few more revisions," he purrs. "Your tread, you know, the distance between the wheels, is such that the car could always be falling off grease racks. There isn't enough road clearance. The oil pan would play pat-a-cake with every bump in the country. The hood seems a smidgen too low. We have what we call an air cleaner extending 12 inches above the sparkplugs. If we made our engine like flapjacks, we might be able to squeeze lower into the car. Unfortunately, we can't."

The chassis engineer is now acting violent. "What," he screams, "are you going to do about cooling in this mess you claim is a radiator? Where will we put shock absorbers in this **** underslung hack? Did your mother ever tell you about banjo-axle housings? Are you going to steer this monstrosity by remote control or isn't it any of my ******* business?" By this time, the chassis engineer has been surrounded by strong, quick young men. He is frothing at the mouth. He is uprooting handfuls of hair. He is blabbering insanely. Only when the head designer assures him that his complaints will be met does he permit himself to be led away.

A lot of things now happen to your dreamboat. The entire body rises, the hood takes on depth and avoirdupois, the rear end is hiked. Frankly, it doesn't much resemble your $25,000 sketch. At that, you have something left besides your money. Remnants remain of a rakish bodyline and its aerodynamic tail. Thus, you look forward eagerly, if somewhat innocently, to the next design step, the wooden model.

The wood model is the same size as the clay model and has an interior in order to try out comfort, space, and accessories. Evidently, you forgot to allow for center pillars and neglected that passengers have heads, but you have become hardened to minor revisions. The body engineer has more emotional equilibrium than the chassis engineer, he starts mad and stays that way. "How many sheets do you break the body into?" he demands. "Where are we expected to weld?" Actually, you hadn't thought about it. You are an artist, you remind him, not a mechanic.

"Don't you know the size of our flat-plate presses?" he growls. "We can't handle hoods that big. Doors can't be hung at that angle. And what's this sticking out at the rear, a fin? What's it for? Looks pretty, huh? A special jig and 10 hours of welding, to hell with it!" Goodbye tail, goodbye fin, goodbye 'advanced streamlining'. From your original design only the charming filigreed grille is intact. The fact offers some consolation. Many's the time in the uproar of getting production settled you have gazed on that grille. Even if the car doesn't look precisely as you had planned, its shining face will be seen and remembered on thousands of highways. Or will it?

So many people have descended on your car that few have made any lasting impression. With regard to the grille, you have noticed one man in particular, a quiet fellow who has been vaguely described as 'from purchasing'. Frequently during the travail he had brought in strangers to inspect the grille. They viewed it from all angles, tested the heft and took samples away. This was indeed flattering, very likely the young man himself had artistic leanings. He knew beauty when he saw it!

One day, near the end of your troubles, the young man 'from purchasing' approaches. After the kicking around you've been getting, you appreciate his politeness. "I sure liked that grille," he says. The past tense tugs at your heart. Had you heard correctly? You inquire. "That's right. We're not going to take it. We checked with our suppliers and find we can get another design for 18 cents less." You stagger backward, maybe you fall. For a small sum like 18 cents the company is going to discard the last fragment of your dream. Surely it isn't true; surely they wouldn't do that to you for a lousy 18 cents.

"Eighteen cents per car based on volume production can mean quite a lot of dough," he informs you laconically. "We've got to watch pennies in this business. How else do you think we could pay you that $25,000?"

suggested Ex should create a body for his latest race car chassis design. Ex returned home with the blueprints for the chassis and soon came up with a neat racing car in his backroom studio from which he had a 1/8-scale clay modelled. He asked the workshops to make a fiberglass cast of the car, but before the project went any further, Ex suffered his attack. Unbeknownst to Ex, colleagues Maury Baldwin, Dana Waterman, Deo Lewton and Len Klemek decided to turn the design into a breathtaking

piece of automotive art. The car had a metal radiator, rubber hoses, sparkplugs and wires, working suspension and steering and hand-painted body and decals. The car took months to complete, and when finished, was then

This beautifully executed 1/8-scale model of a 1960s Indy-style race car was built by Chrysler Design Engineer Dana Waterman for Ex. Based on a Frank Kurtis-supplied chassis drawing and Exner's design, the car featured an Offenhauser engine, working torsion bars, a chrome-plated tubular frame, brake lines from the master cylinder, and working steering box. The scale decals of Exner's favorite number 5 were hand-painted with a 'one hair' brush by Deo Lewton. Others involved in the project were Maury Baldwin and Ex's modeler Len Klemek, along with the styling model shops. The body of the model was severely damaged in a house fire in 1961, but while Ex was working on the Mercer Cobra in Turin in 1964, he turned over the highly detailed model to the renowned Italian model maker Michael Conte. Conte restored the car for very little recompense as a favour to Ex. The model was then kept in the family until 1988 when it was sold at a Detroit auction for $11,000.

hired William (Bill) M Schmidt who used to head the Lincoln/Mercury studio and had been working at Studebaker-Packard, as a temporary replacement, giving him the title Executive Stylist. Bill Robinson told me that politics were involved with the hiring of Bill Schmidt: "Paul Ackerman felt that Cliff Voss, Ex's second-in-command, was a great designer, just too young to become the head of Styling, and he also wanted to keep some control of the design studio, so he hired Schmidt, who was more mature. Consequently, Cliff always felt like somebody's kid brother." Although Ex tried to visit Highland Park as often as possible, Schmidt was gaining confidence and control. It was at this point that Chrysler bosses made a very expensive mistake. Exner planned to introduce his second generation of Forward Look cars for 1958 but Chrysler bosses wanted even more market share, so, against Ex's wishes, they took the decision of pushing the designs through a year early, long before they had been completely engineered.

The 1957 models were released to rapturous applause and drove straight into the history books. The new Chrysler, Dodge, De Soto, Plymouth and Imperial cars constituted the largest group of all-new cars ever to appear in one year from one company. Never before or since, had a motor manufacturer released a completely new range across all of its passenger car divisions. They were quite simply astonishing and took the motoring world and the public by surprise. The all-new '57 models received even longer, lower and wider bodies than the '55 range. They wore soaring tail fins, large glass areas, dual headlamps, low belt-lines and a restrained use of chrome ornamentation. Public response to the new 'swept-wing' styling was very positive and again sales took-off. Some of the success of these cars was due to the low down stance of the car and their even lower hoods. It is thought that Exner fought hard with engineers

mounted on a piece of brick track from Indianapolis and presented to the design chief on his return to work.

Exner returned home to convalesce and under Mildred's watchful gaze, he took things easy, still looking very pale. He took advantage of the time off work and went back to one of his old hobbies of painting fine art pictures and toying with ideas for car designs, but it wasn't any easy time for the designer, especially trying to overcome his addiction to nicotine. Within months he was trying to get back to work and making occasional visits to the studio, sometimes being pushed around in a wheelchair. Colbert forced him to stay home; the designs for the 1957 models through to 1960 were almost done. Exner's administrator, Carl Reynolds, didn't work out, so to oversee control of the Styling Studio while Exner was recuperating, Tex Colbert and Paul Ackerman

Because of the perceived need for secrecy, very few illustrations survive from this period of time. This design for a De Soto four-door sedan, done in 1956 by Jack Kenitz and illustrated by Bill Lucas, carried many styling cues that were carried on to actual production vehicles for 1958 and 1959.

Another rare image is this unsigned suggestion for a 1959 Dodge, drawn in December 1956.

Virgil Exner will always be inextricably linked to the stunning Chrysler Corporation cars of 1957. This was their defining moment. Longer, lower, wider and more graceful than any mass produced American car ever seen, Exner stole General Motors grip on styling and instantly made competitors cars look obsolete.

THE IMPERIAL FOUR-DOOR SOUTHAMPTON

Both the Four-Door Southampton, above, and the Two-Door Southampton, shown below on the opposite page, have the landau-type roof design, which adds a smart note of distinction and individuality. The landau section, defined by the gracefully curved chrome molding, has the same color as the body, with the forward section of the roof finished in a different color.

Dual headlights permit easier control of light patterns—one set for city and both sets for country driving. Optional on Crown and LeBaron, extra on Imperial.

1957 Imperial. Ex strived for many years to get curved side glass on his cars. Finally, engineering and technology caught up with his idea. The Imperial was the first production car to use curved side glass, and would go on to become an industry standard, while all Chryslers offerings used compound-curved windshields, another industry first.

Facing page – Top: Chrysler model #613. Much of the classic 300C styling came from an Exner design coded #613 from October 1955. Seen here as a full-sized clay model, the design developed into a fully-engineered car and carried the 300C badges. The front end treatment in particular would go almost unchanged for the production models; Middle: The full-size clay model of #613 became a fully engineered prototype body. Once again built by Ghia, #613 was shipped to America where it underwent vigorous testing. Only the tail fins, continental spare wheel, and rear lights changed for the production models; Bottom: 1957 Chrysler 300C. This car, more than any other, encompassed the ethos of the Forward Look. No car before, and few since, offered such levels of performance, handling and style in such a classy package. Every other car on the road became immediately obsolete when Chrysler released the 300C.

to get the cars dropped as much as possible, asking them to lose 5in from the 1956 dimensions. Many engineers claimed this was an impossible feat but executive engineer Harry Chesebrough was on his side. Chesebrough and Ex had suffered each other for some time, but after a few years, the engineer came to respect Ex and what he was trying to achieve and the pair became firm friends. Stylists worked with engineers to come up with ways of lowering the overall height. This work was done with a huge

1957 Chrysler. It was all about fins, and this publicity photograph of a pre-production 1957 Chrysler convertible says it all. Clean, simple and canted slightly outwards, it immediately made all other cars seem old-fashioned. (Brett Snyder)

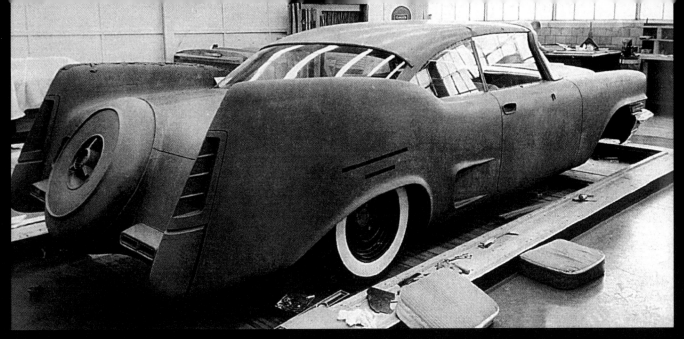

sense of urgency; the team redesigned the manifolds, air filters, and roof lining, and prompted the introduction of 14in wheels and the torsion bar suspension system. The latter innovation allowed the loss of a few precious inches in height and added positively to the handling characteristics. Plymouth stylist Hal Pilky came up with the wider quad headlamp cowling for the front fenders, which transformed the front end of the cars. Ex really liked the look of them and put them on all of the other marques, but it was the simple, stylish fins that set the cars apart from the competition. Virgil junior said, "Father loved those fins. The idea was to get some poise at the rear of the car, to get off of soft, rounded back ends, to get some lightness to the car and draw the observer's eyes upward. The fins were aesthetic but he did believe that they had a functional role to play. He ran tests in wind tunnels and they did work. They moved the center of air pressure

Opposite: "This baby can flick its tail at anything." This advert from 1957 extols the virtues of Exner's all-new De Soto. Note the neat, but problematic, exhaust ports that finish through the rear bumpers.

back, a little closer to the center of gravity, providing more inherent directional stability."

Of all the new cars, the Imperial was arguably the

Main & inset: 1957 wind tunnel De Soto. These two rare images show Chrysler staff carrying out aerodynamic tests on a scale model of a De Soto. Smoke was blown through a small wind tunnel to gauge the efficiency of the overall dart shape. (Brett Snyder)

This baby can flick its tail at anything on the road!

DE SOTO FIREFLITE 4-DOOR SEDAN IN SEATONE BLUE AND WHITE

Take the wheel of a new De Soto, and pilot her out through traffic toward the open road. Before you turn your second corner, you'll know you're driving the most exciting car in the world today. Here are some of the reasons why:

New *Torsion-Aire* ride! You get an amazingly level ride with De Soto's new suspension—Torsion-Aire. You take corners without sway . . . stop without "dive."

New *TorqueFlite* transmission! Most advanced ever built. Gives a smooth flow of power, exciting getaway!

New *Triple-Range* push-button control! Simply touch a button and *go!* Positive mechanical control.

New *Flight Sweep* styling! The new shape of motion— upswept tail fins, low lines, and 32% more glass area.

New super-powered V-8 engines! De Soto engine designs are efficient and powerful! (Up to 295 hp.)

Drive a new De Soto before you decide. You'll be glad you did. De Soto Division, Chrysler Corporation.

Wide new price range . . . starts close to the lowest!

FIRESWEEP—big-value newcomer—priced just above the lowest. 245 hp

FIREDOME—medium-priced pacemaker—exciting performance. 270 hp

FIREFLITE—high-powered luxury—the last word in design and power. 295 hp

DE SOTO

. . . the most exciting car in the world today!

De Soto dealers present **Groucho Marx** in "You Bet Your Life" on NBC radio and TV

95

most elegant and was the one that Ex spent the most time on, almost living in the Imperial studio as one colleague remembered. For the first time, the Imperial was unique; sharing no sheet metal or interior fittings with corporate siblings, but the main innovation was the glass. The 1957 Imperials were the first production cars to use curved side glass as standard, complementing the compound-curve windscreen that wrapped around and over the top of the roof. Engineer Les Parr worked closely with glass manufacturer Pittsburgh Plate Glass (PPG) to make Exner's design a reality, and it was no easy task. The new Chryslers entered with the Windsor and made use of two-tone styling on their rear flanks. The Saratoga made a return after some five years absence to take up the middle price spot and featured more luxurious color-coded upholstery, and a more powerful V8 engine. The New Yorker and 300C were the most expensive offerings from the Chrysler Division, offering luxury and extreme performance. The 300C was perhaps the defining incarnation of everything that was good about the Forward Look style; never before had such a car received such technical and styling autonomy. Its development from model #613 is well documented, but the '57 300C didn't have to share parts with any other car. Its grille was unique,

Because of the speed at which they were developed, the cars for 1957 came with many inherent problems, with Plymouth receiving most of the criticism. Poor fit and finish, along with under-engineered parts, caused leaks, creaks and mechanical failure. A new sound was heard on the highways of America, the sharp retort of a snapping torsion-bar.

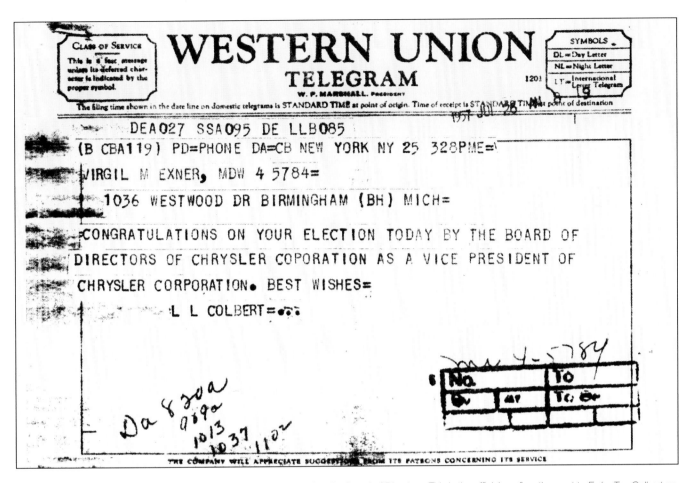

WESTERN UNION
TELEGRAM
W. P. MARSHALL, PRESIDENT

CLASS OF SERVICE
This is a fast message unless its deferred character is indicated by the proper symbol.

SYMBOLS
DL = Day Letter
NL = Night Letter
LT = International Letter Telegram

The filing time shown in the date line on domestic telegrams is STANDARD TIME at point of origin. Time of receipt is STANDARD TIME at point of destination

DEA027 SSA095 DE LLB085

(B CBA119) PD=PHONE DA=CB NEW YORK NY 25 328PME=

VIRGIL M EXNER, MDW 4 5784=

1036 WESTWOOD DR BIRMINGHAM (BH) MICH=

CONGRATULATIONS ON YOUR ELECTION TODAY BY THE BOARD OF

DIRECTORS OF CHRYSLER COPORATION AS A VICE PRESIDENT OF

CHRYSLER CORPORATION. BEST WISHES=

L L COLBERT=

THE COMPANY WILL APPRECIATE SUGGESTIONS FROM ITS PATRONS CONCERNING ITS SERVICE

Thanks to the huge success of the 1957 range, Exner was promoted to the Board of Directors. This is the official confirmation sent to Ex by Tex Colbert on 26th July 1957.

not borrowed from a sibling, minimal ornamentation complemented the stylish body surfaces, and power and handling could not be matched by any other similar car in the world. Exner's functionalistic lines helped the 300C win The Industrial Designer's Institute's award for Excellence in Automotive Design, the car itself becoming an ageless classic. De Sotos now came in four series; the new Dodge-based Firesweep, and the larger Firedome, Fireflite and sporty Adventurer. All De Sotos wore the triple-stack tower rear lights and neat, but impractical exhaust vents that exited through the rear bumper. Undoubtedly, Dodge carried the most flamboyant styling of all the corporations' offerings in 1957. The front grille featured a gullwing-shaped horizontal bar, which dipped in the center and held a large Dodge crest. As with all of the 57 models, they had the deeply recessed headlights, covered by the large eyebrows, but it was the unusual trim on the rear fins that made the Dodge so distinctive. Substantial chrome strips started just under halfway along the car and curved up to separate the top part of the rear fender, giving the impression of a separately mounted fin. Chrysler's biggest

success was the entry-level model Plymouth. The simple beauty of these cars was undeniable and advertising at the time shouted: "Suddenly, it's 1960! ... 3 years ahead... the only car that dares to break the time barrier!" The 762,231 Plymouths sold were enough to knock Buick off its traditional 3rd place in the ratings and helped take Chrysler sales to over 1 million.

Design director Bill Mitchell over at General Motors, caught a glimpse of some Chrysler pre-production models as he drove past a holding pen behind the factory on Mound Road. He returned to his studio, rounded up some stylist and took them right back to the pen. The gathered designers were speechless, realising that they were in trouble. The planned fat, chrome-encrusted cars they had ready for the next three years were no match for the gorgeous Mopars spied through the fence. After leading the industry for decades, GM cars now looked out of date. Mitchell headed a styling revolt against Harley Earl that would totally change the direction of GM styling for many years. While Ex was recovering at home, accolades were being collected for the new range. *Motor Trend*

Above & below: 1957 Chrysler Dart. The Dart was a continuation of the study into aerodynamics that had started in 1955 with the Ghia Gilda. Measuring 223in in length, the Dart shape was perfected by Giovanni Savonuzzi in Europe's largest wind tunnel to ensure maximum aerodynamic ability. The car featured advanced chassis and suspension details, along with a retractable rear windshield that slid into the roof section.

presented Chrysler its Car of the Year award, and the Industrial Design Institute presented the Gold Medallion to Virgil M Exner, Henry T King, H T Bannister, Clifford C Voss, Carl Reynolds, and Robert E Bingman, for the 1957 Chrysler Corp cars. On 19th April, the corporation cars made automotive history again when they won a clean sweep in every available price range and weight class in the 1957 Mobilgas Economy Run. Because of the phenomenal success of these cars, on 25th July, Exner was invited to join the select few members of the board when he was elected to the position of Executive Vice President and Director of Styling, the first person to ever hold that office. This was now the third time that Ex had occupied a freshly created post. Unlike Raymond Loewy, Ex was quick to spread responsibility for the success throughout his team, but Chrysler used Ex (with his debonair character and Gary Cooper movie star good looks) as a marketing tool, putting him in the limelight as often as possible. Away from Chrysler, he became the Vice President of the SAE and once again was asked to speak before them. Still looking quite pale, on 14th September 1957, Ex made a presentation to the Detroit Section

of the SAE about his latest idea car, the Dart, with regard to styling and aerodynamics.

The Ghia-built Dart was an experiment in aerodynamics and by far the most distinctive vehicle from the Chrysler-Ghia partnership. It featured a fully retractable metal hard-top that slid into the trunk beneath the rear window, altering the line of the rear deck, and huge tail fins. Designed in the Advance Styling Studio and overseen by Exner, it was inspired by Italian engineers watching inkblots moving in 200mph winds along the surface of plastic models. The end result was an almost perfect dart shape, reinforcing Exner's belief that fins worked. While it was being built in Italy, aerodynamicist Giovanni Savonuzzi developed the car further from his initial Chrysler-based Ghia Gilda. Extensive wind tunnel and road testing was carried by him before it was shipped to America. When it was shown to the public, Chrysler called it a "hydroplane on wheels" and "the most nearly perfect aerodynamic passenger car design in the world". Originally painted in silver and black, when Chrysler technicians had completed their testing of the 4-passenger Dart at Chrysler's Chelsea Proving Grounds, it was returned to Ghia in early 1957. Ghia replaced the retracting hard-top for a more conventional soft-top,

1957 Dart II. It is not widely known that the Dart idea car had three incarnations. This was the second, and in this configuration the retractable roof had been removed to make it a convertible, but still with high tail fins. Bodywork was now bright red. The car is seen here on the streets of Turin alongside two Fiat-based Ghia Jolly cars.

Few pictures exist of the Dart in its second state. This photo was taken at the Turin Motor Show in 1957, before it was transformed into the Diablo. Ghia did build another Dart-like car in 1958 called the Chrysler 400. This yellow and black car had the Dart body but with an immovable vinyl covered steel roof, and was a fully engineered prototype. It is rumored that Gene Casaroll from Dual Motors bought the car and rebadged it as a Dual, for use as a pre-production model. The Dual-Ghias that did go into production shared no similarities with the Dart or Chrysler 400.

re-worked the incredible fins, and painted it red. The car was then renamed the Chrysler Diablo and sent back to America. The Dart was powered by a Chrysler 392in³, 375bhp V8 taken from the 300 series and was stretched to 223in long, 80in wide, and 54in high including the fins. The presentation to the SAE can be seen as an attempt to justify the fins on the new experimental car and the production vehicles. They did work, however, but only once the vehicle reached speeds over 80mph! Shortly after completing the work on the Dart, Exner introduced Giovanni Savonuzzi to Jack Cheripar at Chrysler Engineering. Cheripar offered the Italian a job in Detroit, and Savonuzzi was glad to leave Italy. Alberta Savonuzzi, the younger of Giovanni's two daughters explains, "My father left Ghia in 1957. I think he was not only interested in the research possibilities he could pursue at Chrysler, but happy to leave Italy due to a personal tragedy. He had two brothers. Alberto, a lawyer, was executed by the SS in 1943. His youngest brother Giorgio, a surgeon, was killed in a climbing accident near Cortina d'Ampezzo in the summer of 1957. His body was never recovered,

even though my father headed search parties from July to November. I think he took the opportunity to leave Italy and get away from this devastating circumstance."

Savonuzzi joined Chrysler and worked with George Huebner as Chief Engineer Automotive Research, and in Gas Turbine Research and Development from 1957 through 1969. Savonuzzi would go on to design the technical and styling aspects of the 1963/64 Chrysler Ghia Turbine Car for Elwood Engle. After years of feeling exploited, and seeing Huebner take the credit for his work, Savonuzzi finally left Chrysler and returned to Fiat.

Such success had its price. Due to the high demand for the 1957 production models, and being under engineered, quality control went almost unchecked. Early rust-out (seen at its worst on Plymouth vehicles), along with squeaks, leaks and knocks from poor fit and finish, cost Chrysler Corporation dearly in reputation. A new noise was frequently heard on the streets of America – the sharp crack of a snapping torsion bar! Going into a recession in 1958 didn't help either. Although quality was improved as time passed, the damage had been done,

1958 Diablo. The last chapter in the Dart's evolution was the Diablo. Repainted, and with trimmed down fins, this is how the car looks today. (Bortz Collection)

The Imperial for 1958 offered cruise control, along with integrated electro-mechanical door locks, both industry firsts. This rare photo taken in a Chrysler dealership shows the fresh new grille, quad headlamps and heavier bumper which distinguished it from the '57 models.

1958 Crown Imperial Limousine. Rather oddly, the Ghia-built Imperial Limousine wore the new 1958 grille, but retained the 1957 bumper. Priced at just over $15,000, only thirty-one of these leviathan vehicles were built for 1958.

Below & right: 1958 Chrysler 300D FI. With such astounding critical acclaim for its 1957 models, Chrysler wanted to keep change to a minimum for the following year. A very mild face-lift saw the introduction of quad headlights across board and trim detailing. This is one of only sixteen Chrysler 300D performance cars that were fitted with a new Bendix fuel injection system. The system proved unreliable and all of the cars were recalled and modified to run with dual four-barrel carbs, although they all retained their unique 300D FI badges. (Richard Starkweather)

Below: 1958 Chrysler. This rear view picture shows how sometimes less is, well ... less. The taillights that had filled the rear bezels on the 1957 models now looked stunted and mismatched, although the rest of the car was still beautifully proportioned.

Above & right: 1958 Plymouth. The Plymouth saw the least change of all of the Corporation cars, the biggest difference being that the lower grille panel, designed by Bill Robinson, now ran horizontally, to match the upper grille. This car, based in England, is painted in non-original red and white, in honour of the Steven King story Christine. *The original color of the 1958 Fury was buckskin beige.*

Below: 1958 Dodge. Once the designs were perfected, they were passed on to professional artists to illustrate. This was how Virgil started out, illustrating at Advertising Artists, Inc in South Bend. Now it was his time to pass work to illustrators. This is a Dom Pacitti picture of the 1958 Dodge convertible. (Brett Snyder)

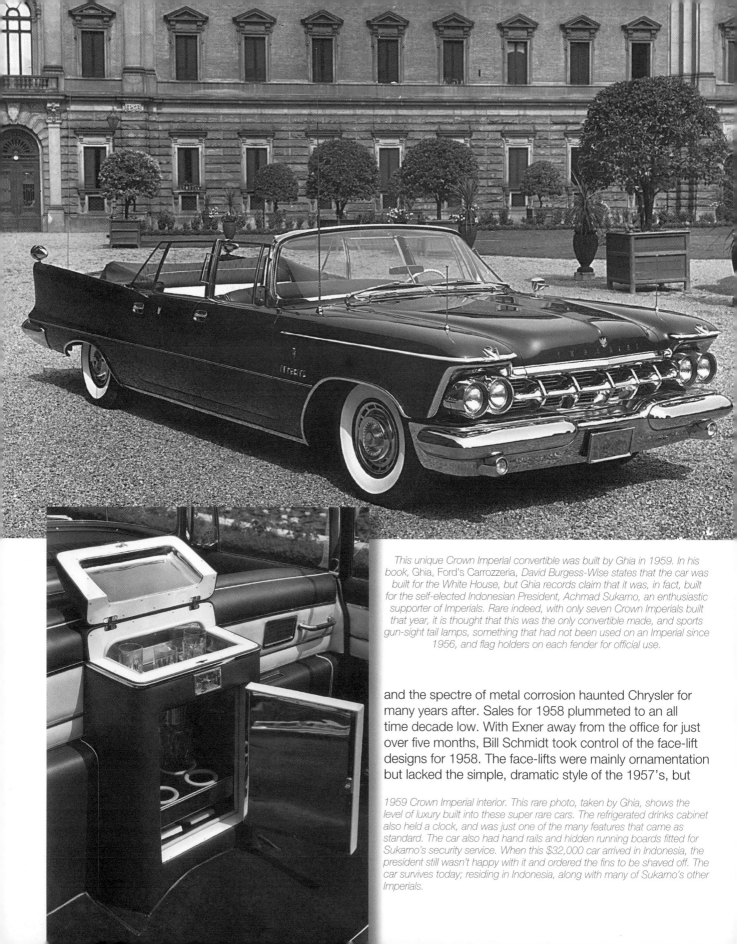

This unique Crown Imperial convertible was built by Ghia in 1959. In his book, Ghia, Ford's Carrozzeria, *David Burgess-Wise states that the car was built for the White House, but Ghia records claim that it was, in fact, built for the self-elected Indonesian President, Achmad Sukarno, an enthusiastic supporter of Imperials. Rare indeed, with only seven Crown Imperials built that year, it is thought that this was the only convertible made, and sports gun-sight tail lamps, something that had not been used on an Imperial since 1956, and flag holders on each fender for official use.*

and the spectre of metal corrosion haunted Chrysler for many years after. Sales for 1958 plummeted to an all time decade low. With Exner away from the office for just over five months, Bill Schmidt took control of the face-lift designs for 1958. The face-lifts were mainly ornamentation but lacked the simple, dramatic style of the 1957's, but

1959 Crown Imperial interior. This rare photo, taken by Ghia, shows the level of luxury built into these super rare cars. The refrigerated drinks cabinet also held a clock, and was just one of the many features that came as standard. The car also had hand rails and hidden running boards fitted for Sukarno's security service. When this $32,000 car arrived in Indonesia, the president still wasn't happy with it and ordered the fins to be shaved off. The car survives today; residing in Indonesia, along with many of Sukarno's other Imperials.

Sharing some styling cues with the ill-fated Norseman, the Imperial D'Elegance was a Ghia-built, full-size mock-up based on a 1958 chassis. Exner was still striving for maximum all-round visibility, and the pillarless windows on this four-door hard-top went a long way toward achieving that goal. The squared front fenders and sculpted side panels were predictive and would be seen on Chrysler Corporation vehicles over the following years. (Ford Archive UK)

there were some improvements. The quad headlamps that had only been legal in some states were now universally available and fitted to all '58s. Bill Robinson, one time member of the famous Ramchargers drag team, was also one of the designers behind the 1957, '58 and '59 Plymouths. I asked him how he felt about the front end styling on the '57 models, which at the time took some criticism. Bill told me that he had come up with a front end design that had horizontal bars above and below the bumper. "Everybody liked that design, they were going to go with that, then Hal Pilky (Plymouth chief designer) went to the New York Auto Show and saw a LaSalle II (GM's show car from the 1955 Motorama) that had a grille that swept under and he fell in love with that. So he came back and he took out that lower part and he put the LaSalle in and I hated that thing. So what finally happened is in '58 they went back to what I originally designed in '57 which took that grille and took it down in below and it looked much better."

Exner came back to work in the winter of 1956 and found the designs for the 1961 range completed but the studio personnel had split into two camps, one firmly behind him and the other backing Schmidt. Because Ex

was still not back to full health, Colbert kept Schmidt on at Chrysler to help with the workload, but the temporary

De Soto celebrated its thirtieth anniversary in 1959 but rumors were running rife that, as a division, its days were numbered. Of all the 1959 cars offered by Chrysler, the De Soto was arguably the best looking, with more subtle use of ornamentation than its stable mates, and clever use of contrasting colors within the full-length sweep-spear side trim.

Below & right: The most flamboyant division of the Chrysler stable, Dodge loaded on the chrome and brightwork to give a much heavier look to what were very quick cars, typified by the deeply hooded eyebrows over the headlamps. This is a Custom Royal Lancer four-door pillarless hard-top, Dodge's flagship for 1959.

replacement had thoughts of a more permanent position. On a personal level, Bill and Ex got on very well, with Schmidt introducing Ex to boating in a big way. The pair spent many weekends at Grosse Pointe Yacht Club where Schmidt moored his powerboat. Ex and Mildred then joined the select club and bought their own 25ft CrisCraft cabin cruiser, mooring it at Grosse Point. At work however, two bosses did not make for a pleasant working environment. On the occasions that Ex had visited his studios while still convalescing, he would direct the various projects as he saw fit. As soon as he left the building, Schmidt would go around, countermand his directions, and leave his own. He also took the opportunity to promote some of his supporters to key positions within the studios, including making Dick Teague Chief Stylist for Chrysler and De Soto. This caused even more resentment between the two factions. The situation was helped somewhat with Exner's promotion to Vice President of Styling but did not deter Schmidt from his

goal of ousting Exner and taking control. Exner worked in his back room studio away from prying eyes. Some of his staff thought that he had become preoccupied and reclusive at this stage, but what they could not know was that Ex was trying to create a fresh new style that didn't include sky-high fins. Cliff Voss recalls, "Ex would see something in the studio he didn't like and would do his own design in his back room studio, and then I'd have to go to the studio to redirect what they were doing. Ex was shy, and I was his fall guy." With the failure of the 1958 models and the criticism that was directed at the face-lift '59 cars, Ex realized that the era of the fin was coming to an end and was keen to see them go. He also had to deal with Schmidt. He formed an idea that harked back to the classical long hood, short deck style of yesteryear. In May 1959, he got Cliff Voss, Bill Brownlie (head of the Imperial Studio) and stylist Dick Baird into his office and said, "Bill, I want you to do a completely unique automobile for me in the Imperial Studio, and I want it done in two weeks. And it has to be done in complete secrecy; no one must see it except us." Brownlie started the very next day and put his team on two 10-hour shifts, with the daytime crew doing the styling and the nightshift working on the clay model. Exner had asked for a full-size, see-through model that had to be fitted with plastic windows and a painted Di-Noc coating (an ultra-thin flexible plastic membrane that when applied, simulated a reflective paint surface and could be sprayed, giving the impression of painted metal), for all intense and purposes, a completely detailed car, made of clay. Timing was critical because Schmidt was due to be away for the next ten days on vacation, and shortly after his return there was a high-level product planning meeting scheduled that would decide the direction that ChryCo cars would follow into the new decade.

The new design was set around a basic Dodge platform and evolved into a neat two-door coupe. Ex directed some of the styling based on the horizontal rear end that he had created for the Ghia L6.4, but made only one dictate; the car must have flush glass-to-body sides. This meant that the side glass would sit almost flush with the door sheet metal at the belt-line, giving a single curved aircraft fuselage look to the model. The team realized that Ex's job might be on the line with this car so they gave it their best shot. Dick Baird oversaw the handover from day to night shift and showed the modelers what was required, and engineer Les Parr created the windows. The car developed through the first week into a 2+2 coupe that featured

1959 Plymouth. Another heavy-handed face-lift for Chrysler's main seller, Plymouth, but the largest bone of contention was the superfluous 'trashcan lid' simulated spare-wheel that proved unpopular with buyers. Many paid extra to get a trunk lid sans spare wheel. Fins continued to grow longer and higher, with Plymouth sporting the largest available from the corporation.

Most designs got no further than the drawing board. This slightly wild idea for a De Soto was designed by Dick Teague and illustrated by Bill Lucas in January 1959, and features a GM-style Parisian flat-top roof and large greenhouse. (From the collections of The Henry Ford)

Design-Teague- Illustration- Lucas-
1 · 29 · 59

1957 Chrysler 375 interior. Named after the power given from its 375bhp Hemi V8 engine, the luxurious coupe came with a push button Torqueflite transmission and a host of power options including electric windows, which were all operated by push buttons. Gauges were held in a white leather-wrapped instrument pod with the push buttons for the automatic transmission situated just to the left of the pod. Rear passengers had individual swivel-type reading lights that were operated by switches on either side of the center console, and front passengers sat close to the Hi-Fi Highway record player, mounted below the dash in the forward center console. Originally painted in Maroon, the car changed hands and colors several times until it was found in a junk yard in 1988, looking very forlorn. It is thought that a collector from Grosse Pointe bought the car, although its current location is unknown. (Ford Archive UK)

Opposite & right: 1957 Chrysler 375. This almost forgotten, but elegant sport coupe, was based on a Chrysler 300C chassis, and was a beautiful blend of Exner's styling and fine Italian workmanship. Built by Ghia, the car seated four people comfortably in soft white leather bucket seats, separated by a small center console.

1959 Plymouth 250 Valiant. This neat little coupe was just one of many one-off prototypes built by Ghia for Chrysler, along with the 275, 375, 400 and Chrysler 500. Designed by Ex, he called it 'gun stock design' owing to the upper front and rear fender line treatment.

Plymouth Super Sport. This was how the executives and Schmidt saw the first Super Sport. The full-size clay model was double-sided; the right side wore a graceful C-pillar that kicked up at the flank and a traditional door with curved side glass, while the left side of the car had a more radical wraparound rear screen and a longer door that cut higher into the roof. The rear end wore two similar but not identical versions of the fresh-looking horizontal fins.

elegant horizontal blades that started at the front fender, continued through the door, and emerged into a flat fin at the rear, which held an oval shaped taillight. Unusual V-shaped windscreens that again were inspired by older classic cars, and fine roof pillars complemented the clean lines. The car was badged as a Plymouth and given the name Super Sport. To ensure the model detailing on the Super Sport was finished, Bill Brownlie worked the last three days on the night shift, but unbeknownst to the team, when Schmidt returned from his vacation he got wind of the 'secret project' going on in the Imperial studio. He let himself in using his own passkey and bawled out the designers working on the car, trying to shut the project down. They refused and he could take it no further. The car, gleaming with its red painted body and shining chrome bumpers, was ready for the 8:30am meeting and impressed the Chrysler top brass. They did a U-turn on the designs currently underway and went for the fresh look of the new car. With this major defeat hanging over him, Schmidt left Chrysler with a six-month contract to work as a consultant on a competitive line, and on the basis of this, he set up his own design business, taking with him some of his supporters from Chrysler. Unbeknownst to Exner, his time at Chrysler was almost over too, when he became the scapegoat for the Vice President's huge mistake.

With a clear plan now in front of them, Exner's designers began work on styling a new range of full-size cars for 1962 for all of the Chrysler divisions, evolving from the Plymouth Super Sport model. By the end of July 1959, a series of full-scale models were built, including four-door sedan and station wagon bodies. Exner's S-series, as they were known, offered a glimpse of hope in a stormy period for the corporation. Ex had already tested this new style on the public when he was asked to create a compact car for release in late 1959 as a 1960 model. This project gave Exner the first true opportunity to utilise his fuselage design and attempt to get the side glass as flush to the door panels as possible, and would also see the precursor to the platform type of design, where body and chassis engineers worked alongside stylists to produce a complete package.

In the mid-'50s, there were strong signs of a change in consumer attitudes. The public was saying that it wanted smaller automobiles, especially when the recession took hold in 1958. To underline this, cars like the small VW Beetle and other foreign imports were selling well, along with the homegrown Rambler, so Chrysler announced that it would build its first compact. Ford and GM were slightly ahead of the game already with work on the Falcon and Corvair well under way. Chrysler

Planned 1962 S series models. The Super Sport spawned a complete series of designs called the S series. These factory photos show some of the designs, including a station wagon, Imperial, Chrysler and De Soto with the Plymouth sitting center stage on the studio turntable.

This proposal for the cancelled 1962 De Soto was created by John Samsen. According to him, this stunning design was inspired by the Dodge FliteWing show car, but the demise of De Soto ended any hope for this beautiful car. (John Samsen)

1960 Valiant. Developed through 1959 in complete secrecy, the Valiant was Chrysler's answer to Ford's Falcon and the Chevy Corvair. This quirky little car was a sales success for Chrysler, and, oddly, predicted where Ex was going with his styling. Odd because he introduced styling cues on the low-priced Valiant that he wanted to float up to the more expensive models, instead of starting at the top and watering down the designs to the cheaper offerings.

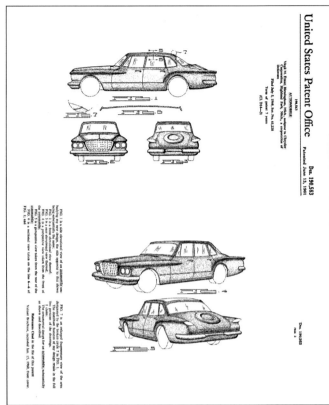

Exner patented the complete design of the Valiant bodywork.

bosses still dragged their collective corporate feet until it was obvious even to them that a sea change in taste was developing. Exner gave Chrysler another huge success with his Valiant. To the many pundits who expected another high-finned, big-engined car, Chrysler's new compact was staggeringly different. As early as April 1957, Chrysler had been thinking about building a compact, and by May 1958 had set up the Small Car Study Program, headed by Harry Chesebrough, to develop a car ready for release in 1962. Shortly after, Chrysler bosses learned that Ford and General Motors were both planning to launch their compacts for the 1960 model year. This really put the cat amongst the pigeons and the planning group began to bicker amongst themselves as to what was to be done. The original plan of building a four-seater that could return 25 to 30mpg and sell for as little as $1850 soon fell by the wayside. In a product planning meeting held on 8th July 1958, Chesebrough and Ex showed two full-size clay models, one with a wheelbase of 106in and the other with a 103in base, both wearing Falcon nameplates. Almost immediately, it became evident that the 106in model was the only viable option. Changes

had been made to the specifications that now asked for seating for six adults, weight had increased by 400lb over the initial recommendation and fuel economy had dropped significantly down to 22mpg. The committee gave the go ahead for the new car to be developed for production.

By the end of July, a team of more than two hundred engineers and designers had moved into 403 Midland Avenue, and then worked in complete secrecy to develop the new car. "Ex was intensely involved in the development of the Valiant," recalls Bill Brownlie. "He wanted an elegant look as opposed to cheap, thus the six-window roof and Ferrari mouth." Other Chrysler employees not involved in the project were told that the team were working on a special defence contract, which was not unusual at Chrysler. By August 1959, the job was

Opposite top: 1960 Valiant V-200. The Valiant initially sold as a separate marque, only becoming a Plymouth sub-series in 1961. Offered in two lines; the base V-100 and more luxurious V-200. The V-200 was easily identified by the stainless steel strip that ran from behind the front wheel opening to the rear of the car.

Opposite bottom: 1960 Valiant. All of Exner's styling themes were apparent on the Valiant; sculpted body, fully open wheelarches, large greenhouse, long hood and short deck, and the ubiquitous trash can spare wheel stamp on the trunk. Mid-year saw the addition of a four-door estate version followed in 1962 by a two-door coupe.

Opposite: This was the flagship for the Chrysler Corporation for 1960, the Imperial convertible. Although the other divisions introduced uni-body construction for the start of the new decade, Imperials continued to be built on a traditional chassis.

1960 Chrysler. This beautiful illustration, done by Michael Cody, shows how the sharper fins now start just behind the A-pillar.

complete with the first car rolling off the production line just one month later. Throughout its development, the new compact continued to be called the Falcon, after Exner's previous idea car from 1955, but Henry Ford II wanted the name for Ford's new compact. Ford approached Tex Colbert and asked if they could have the name. Virgil Jr states that Tex approached Ex to ask how he felt about giving Ford the name. "Well, I guess they do us some favors once in a while", he replied, "and we do them some favors, so that's ok." But Junior also says that his father came up with the replacement name of Valiant. "Back in those days, marketing, advertising and design came up with the names of the cars. Father always liked Prince Valiant, the comic strip. It was one of his favorite comic strips because of how well it was drawn by the artist Hal Foster. So he decided it would be neat to have Valiant as the name of the car." This goes against archive records that suggest Chrysler conducted extensive polling of customers, asking them to come up with a name for the new car. From over two thousand suggestions, a short list was reduced to just five names, with the Valiant coming out on top.

However it was named, the Valiant arrived in dealerships in October 1959, interestingly as a marque of its own, and it was not until 1961 that it became a Plymouth in America (although it became a Chrysler in export markets, except for Canada where it remained its own marque). The cars, all built at the Dodge plant in St Louis, Missouri, were all four-door sedans and featured typical Exner touches that were inspired by European styles: the radiator-sized front grille, radiused wheelarches, sports-deck trunk lid, and classic long-nose and short rear-deck proportions. The distinct Valiant body style was set using crisp blade-like lines on the front fenders that were matched at the rear, culminating in oval shaped taillights. Exner wanted to see a continuous curve from the roof down to the sills, which required thinner doors and almost flush window-to-door fitment. Odd-looking perhaps, but they were incredibly successful. Priced between the Falcon and Corvair, out of the three the Valiant was the best engineered, the best handling and the quickest, but high sales of 180,000 units in its first year could not match Ford's 417,000 Falcons. The Valiant was

fitted with a radical new 170in^3 slant six that gave 101bhp in its basic form, fitted to a 3-speed manual gearbox as standard or as a cost option, the new, smaller Torqueflite 904 automatic gearbox. This lighter box was made from aluminum and was activated by Chrysler's famous push-button changer. Underneath the Uni-body shell sat torsion bar front suspension and rear leaf springs. The whole body of the car underwent a seven-dip rust proofing sequence before receiving two coats of 'Lustre-bond' enamel paint.

The Valiant was a big hit for Chrysler in an otherwise glum year, but even more overlooked than its sales success was its amazing achievement at the track; the mid-season release of a hyper-package boosted horsepower up to 148bhp, giving racers power a plenty. The package consisted of a long, tuned ram intake manifold, 4-barrel carb and dual-exhaust manifolds. With tweaking, engineers were able to squeeze up to 185bhp from some race engines. The results were incredible; on 31st January 1960, NASCAR held its inaugural 'Compact Car Division' race at Daytona. Led by Lee Petty, the seven Valiants entered took the first seven places across the line in the ten lap race, then three Valiant's driven by Marvin Panch, Roy Schecter and Larry Frank finished 1st, 2nd and 3rd position in the main twenty lap race in front of a televised audience. They reached speeds of 122mph! When the Valiant did the same thing the following year, NASCAR cancelled the series. Success in the United States and Canada for the gutsy little car soon spread to other Chrysler strongholds. Australia and South Africa were particularly successful for the car and can still be found in regular use in South African townships as taxis, etc. By the end of the sixties, the Valiant was fighting the VW Beetle for top seller in both of these overseas markets.

The rest of the 1960 line-up was a mixed bag. All of the 1960 cars, except Imperial, were using the new uni-body construction method, but overall dimensions changed little. Uni-body construction replaced the

1960 De Soto. Almost a twin to the Chrysler, De Soto was now in its last full year of production, and only came in two models, FireFlite and Adventurer.

The Polara was Dodge's top-of-the-range offering for 1960, and this Polara hard-top was arguably one of the nicest-looking station wagons ever produced. Sales for all Dodge station wagons topped 51,600 units.

The most dubious styling was seen on the 1960 Plymouth. Shown here in convertible form, the tail fins reached higher and the scalloped front end looked disjointed. They still managed to sell 7080 Fury Convertibles like this one, however.

traditional body-on-chassis method, in an attempt to reduce knocks, squeaks, and leaks. Styling was told that it had to use the same dimensions for the newer vehicles, which is why they look so similar to 1959 cars, even though they shared no body-panels. Plymouth fins grew larger and the front of the car now had awkward, painted-in scallop shapes on the front fenders accentuated with stainless steel trim. Imperial fins got higher and the front end treatment looked heavier. Chrysler and the doomed De Soto fared better and looked lighter than the previous year's offering but it was Dodge which came off the best. Fins stopped short of the rear fenders and were shown at their best on the new Dart Phoenix. For 1961, design took a nosedive; Chrysler and De Soto silhouettes looked similar but the front grilles carried odd inverted trapezoidal headlamps. The Imperial fins grew to ridiculous heights and had the added anguish of having to carry Exner's freestanding headlamps held in large chrome pods, the neo-classic styling lost on the leviathan car. Again

Dodge fared better but not without upset. Buyers of the Dart range complained of safety issues when it became apparent that following cars could not see the indicator/stop lights clearly. By the spring, Darts were being fitted with extra, round nacelles, further up and inward on the rear, to counteract the criticisms, while the earlier cars were retrofitted with the new lights if the owners wished. Dodge also introduced its Valiant-based compact, the Lancer, in 1961, but it was Plymouth which fielded by far the strangest offering for that year. With a front end

By far the most outlandish Imperial has to be the 1961 offering. As well as the introduction of strange front and rear lights, fins reached their zenith this year on the Imperial. The FliteSweep Deck Lid, as the spare wheel cover was called, was an option on all Imperial models.

that was originally designed as a rear end treatment, the puzzled-looking Savoy, Belvedere and Fury struggled to sell. Units sold were half of that from just two years previous. True, the huge fins were gone, the tail-end was clean except for the bullet-type rear lights, but the sour-faced front grille, and scalloped quad headlamps did not prove popular. Because of Exner's absence, Cliff Voss was held responsible for this design nightmare, although he tried to pass the blame for the unpopular styling onto Homer LeGassey.

On his return to work, Exner did agree with Bill Schmidt on one thing, they both disliked the cars for 1961. Some of the show cars fared worse than the production models. The Imperial D'Elegance was a mismatch of styles taken from several previous themes. The Norseman-like front fenders looked ill at ease with the flared fins and Dodge taillights at the rear, topped with small microphone type indicators. The full-width grille made the car look even heavier and clumsier. The Plymouth Cabana, although mildly less wacky than the ill-conceived Imperial D'Elegance, still showed a total disregard for continuity of style. Chrysler styling had lost its sense of direction just as General Motors seemed to rediscover its. Designer John Samsen worked in the De Soto studio throughout this time. He told me: "Ex got us gathered around and asked us where we should be going with styling. Nobody came up with anything. He said, 'Ok, we stick with fins until we come up with something better.'"

Although Cliff was undoubtedly responsible for some of the more bizarre aspects of the 1961 cars, Ex must take some of the responsibility. Cliff was in constant

Exner's controversial freestanding headlamps were introduced in 1961 and would remain an Imperial feature until Elwood Engle restyled the complete car in 1964.

contact with Ex while he was recuperating from his heart attack, and although Cliff had his own thoughts on how cars should look, Ex's influence was great. It is hard to imagine anyone but Virgil Exner creating the Imperial head and tail lamps.

Ghia built two important 'idea cars' for Chrysler during this turbulent period: the Plymouth XNR 500 and the Dodge FliteWing. The XNR ranks as one of the best Exner designs of all time, and was named by the design team in honour of its leader. Mechanically it was based on the Valiant and shared some of its styling, too, but this was a unique car, and not just another idea car. Ex hadn't forgotten the disappointment of not getting his 1955 Falcon into production, and still wanted to build a limited production sports car for Chrysler to go up against the Corvette and Thunderbird. This sensational car had an offset speed bump on the driver's side, which fared into the windscreen and cowl, and continued after the cockpit into a large asymmetrical fin, the front of which made up the backrest for the driver. There was no matching scoop or fin for the passenger's side, giving the XNR the appearance of having an offset driver's position, a feature of many Indy cars at that time. Although it had the look of a single-seat racer, a lower passenger seat and movable race windscreen lay neatly underneath a metal tonneau cover. The front bumper and grille were in a simple, one-piece oval that held a fine mesh grille and quad headlamps, but it was the rear view that was the most eye-catching. A large integrated chrome cross slashed the rear end, with the top part of the vertical line starting at the top of the fin, dropping down to below the level of the exhaust outlets, while the horizontal line made up the rear bumper. The rear was finished off with a large, round gas-filler cap holding the letters 'XNR', which sat adjacent to another flush-fitted metal tonneau that covered a sizeable stowage

The end of an era: the Chrysler 300G would be the last finned 300 to be built. The following year saw the introduction of the 'plucked chickens' as Exner described them, along with the start of the 300 non-letter series cars, a ploy to promote sales of Chrysler's mid-priced cars on the merits of its performance vehicle, as had been done with the Dodge D-500 in 1956. This car is part of Chrysler UK's historical collection.

Above & top right: The 1961 range was designed predominantly by Cliff Voss, although he tried to pass the blame for the unpopular styling to Homer LeGassey. Even Bill Schmidt didn't like them. This Dart shows how odd the styling had become. Strange fins that curved back on themselves created a stunted look at the rear, while the concave grille gave an anguished look to the front.

area. The beauty of this car was not just aesthetic; it was affordable and easy to produce. Utilizing the Valiant's new slant-six but with a high-performance package bolted on, it made the lightweight car almost race ready but street legal, and could probably have been assembled on the Valiant production line. It is thought that, had it gone into production, discerning buyers would have had to pay no more than $3000 for it, much less than the $5840 spent on a Chrysler 300F. Ex was understandably pleased with the outcome. He said that the Plymouth XNR stressed the real focus of an automobile as a true driver's machine with emphasis on special, but not radical, high-performance engineering features. Designer Dick Burke recently told me that they had been getting a consistent 140mph out at the proving grounds but Ex wanted the car to go faster. "He

The Plymouth was the unluckiest recipient of Cliff Voss' styling. The main body of the cars were simple and delightful, with finely shaped rear fenders. Unfortunately, a design that had been created as a rear end treatment was chosen to go on the front, giving the car a very sour-faced look. Sales for all divisions, except Chrysler, plummeted.

By 1959, the Falcon had developed into the XNR. This never-before-seen sketch by Virgil Exner shows his first interpretation of what would become the Plymouth XNR 500. Note that the front view still carries the Falcon name. (From the collections of The Henry Ford)

wanted me to design a steel top for the XNR and a front end for it with an aerodynamic nose. In the end, I only did the nose cone out of fiberglass. There was no opportunity to test it in the wind tunnel so I just built a mouth below the nose cone and put in a bigger, shrouded radiator with two electric fans. That mouth was so low you couldn't even see the opening unless you got way down on it, and we took it out to the PG, I remember, and it went about 153mph. He was delighted when that thing broke 150."

Ex said much the same thing when interviewed years earlier: "After we showed it around a bit, we took it to the road test people. The laboratory really hopped up the engine, to 250hp, a tremendous amount of power. We took it to the proving grounds and had a professional drive it. He lapped at 151 or 152mph, which wasn't bad at that time." No stranger to high speed driving himself, it is thought that he once drove the XNR up to 135mph, this just a few years after his heart attack! The positive response gained at auto shows led Chrysler's Product Planning to put a team together to draw up plans for production for the 1962 season, while Ex developed the styling characteristics. In the June 1961 issue of *Motor Life* magazine Chrysler offered a rendering of how its new sports car would look. "Projected Chrysler sports car shows similarities to XNR" read the caption below the sketch, and went on to point out that some XNR features like external mufflers and a full-sweeping headrest would be dropped, but the rest of the car's styling, including the

As with all of the Ghia-built 'idea cars', the XNR design was sent to Italy in the form of drawings and a plaster model. The Ghia craftsmen then produced a wooden mannequin which would be used as a buck for shaping sheet metal. (From the collections of The Henry Ford)

Left & below: The 1960 XNR 500 was another idea car built by Ghia of Turin. An experimental two-passenger sportscar that was constructed on a modified Valiant chassis, Exner put a great deal of time and effort into this design. Its asymmetrical styling echoed his deep interest in motor racing, and the car wore many sporting features, including competition fuel filler cap, race car cockpit and windshield, and knock-off wheel hubs. The colors used were the reverse of Ex's preferred combination with red bodywork and black leather interior.

PLYMOUTH

When Chrysler Engineering refused to support Exner's proposed XNR sportscar project, Ghia took up the mantle and built the Asimmetrica. Using the same wooden mannequin that it had used for the Chrysler idea car, it developed the idea and added a conventional windshield and full fabric top, while trimming down the rear fin. Along with its steel hard-top sister, the St Regis, the Asimmetrica was shown at many European motor shows, trying to attract financiers who would partner Ghia in a limited production series. No backers were found but it is thought that as many as twenty-five cars were produced before Luigi Segre gave up on the idea of this neat little sportscar. (Brett Snyder)

The 1961 FliteWing was at the forefront of Exner's attempt to redesign the 1962 model range. Built on a standard 118in wheelbase production chassis, the FliteWing wore crisper, more sculpted body lines with the upper portion of the doors cut deep into the roof, to allow for easy access and egress. Styling secretary, and boyfriend of studio engineer Dana Waterman, Judy Warra models the FliteWing idea car. Judy was seen in many of the publicity photos of the time.

grille and hood scoop, survived intact. Unfortunately, the XNR was another casualty of the corporate shenanigans going on at that time and was never built, the official line being that the design was deemed too radical. Chrysler fans would have to wait until the late nineties and the release of the Prowler to get a production two-seater. It is hard to keep a good idea down, though, and in 1961, Ghia built another, slightly different XNR for itself; called the 'Plymouth Asimmetrica', this one had a convertible roof, and was swiftly followed by the St Regis hard-top clone. Both were shown at major European motor shows in the hope of finding a manufacturer willing to produce and sell the low-priced sports car, but to no avail. It is believed that twenty-five copies of the Asimmetrica were built. As for the original XNR, Chrysler eventually sold it to a private individual in Geneva, Switzerland who then sold it to the Shah of Iran in the late-sixties. By 1972 it was in the hands of Kuwaiti car dealer Anwar al-Mulla, where, it is hoped, the car still survives.

The 1961 Dodge FliteWing experimental car, although much larger, was again very much based on the new Valiant and its sibling Dodge Lancer design, and used the styling that Exner hoped to see in the 1962 production vehicles. Sharp, finless fenders and a low truncated belt-line that stopped before the door and restarted just after, gave a sculpted profile accentuated by a hood that was

No doubt the most bizarre Exner car ever built was this hunting car. Built by Ghia for the King of Saudi Arabia, it was based on a 220.1in wheelbase, 1961 Chrysler New Yorker Station Wagon chassis. The car wore 300G badges and a huge cheese cutter emblem in the center of the grille. (Ford Archive UK)

When the extra row of seats was folded forward, a large soft-top convertible roof could be raised for normal use. With the rear-most seats in the elevated position, and the flip-down front screen lowered, hunters had a clear line of fire. (Ford Archive UK)

And no self-respecting dedicated hunting car would be complete without built-in gun racks, of course! (Ford Archive UK)

longer than the rear deck and a bold shield-shaped grille. The FliteWing was a fully functioning vehicle fitted with a 383in³ cross-ram V8 and had easy access and egress for the occupants as its main theme. Two power-assisted flip-up gullwing windows rose when the door handle was touched and remained open until the door was closed, when they would close down automatically. A rubber strip switch was fitted to the lower edge of the windows so that, if fingers were caught when they were descending, an automatic reverse operation started. Inside the car, four lightweight aluminum bucket seats gave a cockpit-like feel and driver information was emphasized with a modern-looking instrument panel that gave updates on fuel, engine temperature, amperage, and oil pressure, along with turn signals, full-beam indicator, and parking brake light. It is reputed to have cost almost $125,000 to develop the FliteWing and was to be the penultimate Exner 'idea

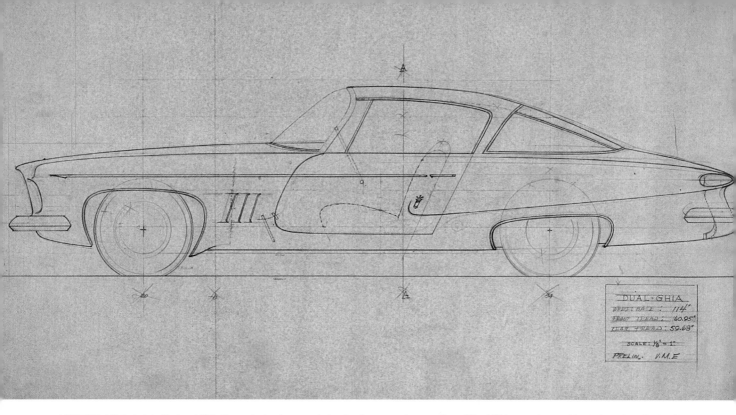

1960 Ghia L6.4 sketch. During 1959, Ex worked out a new design for the second-generation of Dual-Ghia cars. It was this design, done for his friend Paul Farago, that inspired Ex to develop his ill-fated S-series cars for 1962, although some of the styling cues were seen on the 1961 Dodge Polara and Plymouth cars. (From the collections of The Henry Ford)

car' to be built by Ghia for Chrysler. The relationship between Segre and Ex was the keystone to the success of the Chrysler-Ghia partnership, which contributed to the sharing of ideas and designs that travelled in both directions across the Atlantic, creating cars that were neither American nor Italian in design or execution, but something new and exciting. Something we take for granted in today's era of international design, engineering, and manufacturing, but in the 1950s, the Chrysler Ghias were unique.

In 1961, Ex penned the restyling of the Dual-Ghia, which was finalized by Paul Farago. Immortalized by the toy maker Corgi with its ¹⁄₄₃-scale die-cast model. The 1962 L6.4 was again based on Chrysler components but unlike the earlier Duals, completely assembled in Turin. 26 cars of this type were built including the prototype. Named after the 383.2in³ V8's 6.4-litre displacement, the prototype featured a slightly lower roofline and a Dual-Ghia emblem, whereas the production cars wore an L6.4 badge between American and Italian flags. The sleek coupe had a beautifully crafted center console separating the two leather-upholstered bucket seats.

Throughout this time, Exner's health was not good,

1962 Ghia L6.4. The second generation Dual-Ghias were produced between 1960 and 1963, but only twenty-six were built, including the slightly lower prototype. (Brett Snyder)

124

Left to right: Virgil Exner, William L Mitchell of General Motors, and George W Walker from Ford Motor Company pose at the Detroit Motor Show. These three men were the driving force behind American production car design through the 1950s and '60s.

and his family constantly tried to get him to take it easy, but he knew just how important his line-up for 1962 would be. In the late summer of 1959, Ex suffered a crushing blow from Colbert's second-in-command, William C Newberg. It is believed that Newberg was playing golf with Chevrolet's chief, Ed Cole, at the Oakland Hills Country Club north of Detroit, on a sunny Sunday afternoon, when he overheard a conversation Cole was having. He thought he heard Cole say that he was downsizing all Chevrolets for 1962, when in fact Cole was talking about the introduction of the compact Chevy II. Armed with this dangerous piece of misinformation, Newberg rushed to work the following Monday in a panic and ordered an immediate reduction in size of Plymouth and Dodge, and scrapped the new design for the other divisions. In

a meeting with Ex and Chief Engineer Paul Ackerman, Newburg told them to adapt the current design to fit a smaller, 116in chassis instead of the planned 119in base, and to narrow the cars to 72in. The chaos that ensued saw Styling working around the clock to re-jig the designs to fit the new parameters, the night shift doing one thing and the day shift working on its own interpretation, with a half hour overlap for consultation. Eventually, designs were agreed upon but, sadly, the new dimensions stole the proportions needed to carry off Exner's proposed new look, along with the large expanse of curved side glass and wraparound bumpers. What remained seemed stunted and without finesse; the models appearing like slightly larger Valiants. Exner's much-loved Super Sport turned into a parody of its former self and was dropped

125

1962 Chrysler ad. When Chrysler released its 1962 range at the end of September 1961, Exner called them 'plucked chickens' and refused to take responsibility for them.

The 1962 Imperial body went unchanged, except the fins were gone and there was a revised grille, although the suspended headlamps remained. This beautiful example is one of only five hundred and fifty-four Imperial Custom convertibles made that year. (David Munson)

completely along with designs for the all-new De Soto, Imperial, and Chrysler. The Chrysler and Imperial remained virtually unchanged from 1961 except for the shaving off of their fins, dramatically altering their look, while the De Soto Division closed its doors for good in November 1960 with a production of just over 3000 units of the 1961 model completed. In the final product-planning meeting held in the styling showroom, Ex uncharacteristically lost his temper with the Chrysler executives. Cliff Voss recalls, "Exner got really mad at them. 'These cars are plucked chickens,' he screamed. 'They are not competitive and Styling should not be held responsible.'" But, almost inevitably, the department was held responsible.

Exner's power-base was slipping away from underneath him and he could see the end coming. On 28th April 1960, amidst falling sales, Tex Colbert, Ex's main supporter at Chrysler, handed over the presidency to William C Newberg as he moved up to the position of Chairman. Newberg lasted only 64 days in the job and was drummed out over conflict of interest charges. This would be the start of protracted legal arguments for the corporation as Newberg came back with counter claims against Colbert. Colbert resumed the role of President, and kept the chair, but was deeply harmed by some of the accusations thrown at him. On 27th July 1961, Tex Colbert resigned as President and Chairman of the Board, and quietly took up the post of Chairman of Chrysler

As can be seen by this period ad for the Dodge Dart, styling for 1962 evolved directly from the Valiant, not what buyers wanted. Ex introduced styling cues on the cheapest car available, and tried to take that style upward through the price range. Potential buyers saw cheap car styling for more money: it didn't work.

Look at Plymouth now!

1962 Plymouth ad. Exner's abortive restyle is most obvious on the Plymouth. Newberg ordered Dodge and Plymouth to be downsized when he misheard GM bosses saying they were going to downsize for 1962. Exner's delicate balance of style and proportion was lost on the shrunken cars.

Canada until his retirement in 1965. On the same day as Colbert's resignation, accountant Lynn A Townsend was installed as President, with George H Love from the Pittsburgh-based Consolidated Coal Company – and a member of Chrysler's board since 1958 – taking up the position of Chairman just a few months later.

The 1962 cars debuted in late 1961 and, just as Ex had predicted, were a sales disaster for the company. Sales of Plymouth, Chrysler's backbone division, continued to plunge, while Dodge introduced a full-size car in mid-year to help boost its flagging sales. Based on the Chrysler Newport, the Custom 880 did little to assist the downward trend. Townsend was well aware of the stillborn '62s and who was responsible, and assured Exner that his job was safe. However, mounting pressure from a demoralised dealership network could not be ignored; they were calling for a sacrifice. To make Exner's situation even more precarious, Townsend disagreed with the direction that Ex was taking with styling. In retrospect, it was unwise for Ex to debut major styling changes on an economy-priced car like the Valiant and then feed that design upward to the higher-priced

These two sketches, done in 1962, show that Ex did continue to work on Chrysler styling as a consultant, long after he was pushed aside by Townsend. This attractive Chrysler fastback coupe was a proposal for the 1965 model year.

offerings. The fickle, car-buying public would inevitably see low-priced styling on their expensive car, not the other way around. By comparison, General Motors would release a feature on a futuristic concept car, which would then be seen shortly after on a Cadillac, thereafter on a Buick, and so on down the corporate ladder. Exner's backward approach surely could not have helped

Chrysler sales. In late November 1961, Townsend called Ex into his office and told him he was to be replaced as Vice President of Styling. He would be kept on as a consultant until he reached retirement age in 1964 but in essence, he had just been unceremoniously fired. Ex was livid; having followed company instructions to the letter, he found himself being made the scapegoat. There

Radical styling was a complete departure for the last Chrysler Ghia show car to be influenced by Exner. The 1961 Turboflite was designed for Chrysler's Turbine program and featured a highly sculpted body and large jet-fighter-inspired, one-piece cockpit cover. The front grille and lights echoed the new Valiant-based Dodge Lancer. The top was supposed to operate electrically, but after struggling with the problem for many hours, the engineer responsible, Dana Waterman, gave in and fitted screw jacks.

our creativity flourish. Some people are very good at handling creative people and some are not, they're too rigid. Now Engel, he was the opposite, he was brash, and his language was so vulgar, I couldn't talk with him. I remember one time, we came back from lunch and there was a fire axe sticking out of one of the models we were working on, he certainly got his message across that he didn't like it!"

The last Chrysler idea car that Exner had any influence over was his contribution to the turbine project.

The instruments were tightly clustered together on the dash and sat behind a deep dish steering wheel. Seating for four people was provided by light aluminum-framed bucket seats that flanked the transmission tunnel. Note the oversized pedals; the Turboflite was a non-runner, fitted with a dummy turbine engine.

was little he could do. Within days, Townsend had hired Ford designer Elwood Engel as the new VP for Styling. Frustratingly for Exner, the cars that he had already designed for 1963 were a great success and sales for all divisions increased dramatically, although credit would initially go to Engel. The freshly styled Dart and Valiant and uncluttered Chryslers were particularly impressive and showed that Ex was a lot more than a one trick pony.

As a consultant, he kept an office in the main administration block in Highland Park, well away from Styling and Engineering, and did have some minor influence on the 1964 and 1965 cars, but Engel now ruled. The new VP smoothed out the sculpted sides and started a period of slab-sided styling at Chrysler that would stay until the 1990s. Bill Robinson, designer of the 1959 Plymouth, was at Chrysler when Engel took over as Styling Chief and remembers that he changed the whole dynamic of the studio. "For a creative person, Ex was a delight to work for because he was willing to look at anything, and because you had that freedom of expression you were willing to try new and sometimes bizarre things, and you knew he wouldn't knock you down for it, although he might chuckle a little bit. He let

He and Giovanni Savonuzzi worked together with Maury Baldwin, who by this time was head of the Advanced Styling Studio, and designer Jack Kennets to create the Turboflite. Although this dream car was just a push-along mock-up, it was the Turboflite that grabbed the lion's share of press exposure on its tour of all the major auto shows around the world through 1961 and 1962. "Tomorrow is already here" harked the accompanying advertising and, although outlandish in its looks, the Turboflite did indeed proffer cues that would be seen on

The last Exner designed ChryCo production car that he would own was his 1963 Custom Imperial four-door hard-top, which he used as his daily driver until 1972. As with almost all of his company cars, it was black with a red interior. Just before he officially retired from the corporation, he bought a tan, V8-powered 1964 Plymouth Belvedere station wagon for the business he had set up with Virgil Jr.

future Chrysler cars, like the rear spoiler and full-width brake lights seen on late-sixties Dodge and Plymouth cars. Ex may have been involved but it is hard to see how he rationalized the Buck Rogers styling he loathed so much but used liberally on this car. Although it may not have had an engine, everything worked. The large wing on the rear of the car was also functional not only as a spoiler but also housed an aircraft-like airbrake flap. Dana Waterman was the engineer responsible for making all of the hydraulic and electrical systems function. "The Turboflite had a fake turbine engine in it," he told me recently. "It was never intended to be fired up, after the body design was done we asked Ex about putting an engine in there and he said no, we could do without it, but I came up with the air brakes on the Turboflite, to catch the air and slow it down and I had to get everything powered up so we used rows of batteries. But that airbrake went the wrong way, if we had used it, it would have lifted the rear end clear off the ground!" Its radical features included a sleek wraparound windshield, which was incorporated into a transparent semi-bubble top with reverse slant rear window. The entire canopy rose automatically by hydraulics as doors were opened and the interior was lit by an eerie green lighting system. The taillights incorporated amber caution lights, which glowed whenever the driver took his foot off the gas pedal. Front wings left the wheels almost fully exposed, and this unusual design featured built-in landing gear type retractable headlights. The very unusual tires on this car had two white-walls, one on the sidewalls and one in the center of the tread.

When the idea car had finished its tour of duty on the show circuit and testing had finished, Chrysler had the choice of keeping the car but paying a hefty import tax, sending it out of the country or destroying it. As with most of the 'idea cars' built by Ghia, sadly the Turboflite was destroyed when it came to the end of its show career.

Just a few weeks after being fired from Chrysler, the Exner family suffered another tragedy. Marie Exner explains: "We left to go and spend the holidays with my grandparents in South Bend two days before Christmas. On December 22nd, Geoffrey Hicks, the son of Dr Fred Hicks, our next-door neighbor, was shovelling snow on the drive when he realized that our house was ablaze. The fire started in my father's studio; a workman had come to fix the wall heater in there and as soon as he finished we left for Indiana, but the fire must have been smoldering away. Before we left, my mother said to my father that she thought she could smell something burning, but my sister Bronwen said that the smell was probably due to her using curling tongs, so my father locked up and we drove away." After calling the Fire Department, Dr Hicks phoned Ex. On hearing the news, the family returned immediately to find the studio was almost completely gutted and extensive fire and smoke damage to the rest of the house. The family had to move into rented accommodation for several months while the house was rebuilt. Along with most of his work in progress, Ex lost almost all of his sketches and designs from the last twenty-five years as well as a pair of huge medieval swords, the Indy racing car model built by Dana Waterman and a beautiful bronze statue of Joan d'Arc that he adored. Deeply upset but unperturbed, Ex replaced his drawing board and equipment and got straight back into what he had been working on before the fire. His passion for boating and cabin cruisers had grown to a point where he wanted to try to design some for himself. The many hours he had spent cruising around the Great Lakes and up to Canada had given him ample opportunity to research what was fashionable on the water.

Exner realized early on that he lacked the required technical boat building skills needed if he was going to have any success in this field. In the spring of 1962, Ex met with Robert (Bob) W Hobbs, hull designer of some of

By Virgil Exner

Breakthrough in powerboat design

Here's a fresh approach to exterior styling that makes some "new" boats look antiquated. The designs (on these eight pages) may look "too advanced" to some boatmen, but those who value originality will enjoy this preview of a trend

Dynamic lines at once reflect the character of this 38′ express cruiser. She's fast—50 mph—and she looks it. (Twin 350-500 hp engines are recommended.) Air-flow design produces a remarkable integration of hull and superstructure. Strictly a man's boat, she is fitted out below in leather and stainless steel. The new firm of Exner-Hobbs Associates created this design, and those that appear on the following pages.

In the July 1962 issue of Popular Boating *magazine, Exner and Hobbs offered a fresh approach to exterior styling that made new boats look antiquated. Six boats of various sizes were previewed with this 38ft Express Cruiser opening the article. Drawn long before the days of political correctness, this boat was described as 'strictly a man's boat'. The original drawing still hangs in Virgil Exner Jr's home.*

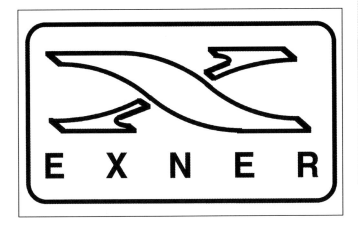

Exner tried to use the letter X wherever he could, developing it into his logo. This was how it looked when Exner Inc opened its doors for business.

In the spring of 1962, Ex met with Robert (Bob) W Hobbs, hull designer of some of the first 'cigarette' powerboats and propulsion systems. They shared a mutual appreciation for each other's talents and got on very wel. Bob Hobbs became part of the team and, together with Virgil Jr, they created Exner-Hobbs Associates. (From the collections of The Henry Ford)

With a clear unity of design, this rakish 18ft sports runabout visually defied its length, looking lower and longer than it is. Planned for molded plastic construction, the longitudinal skylight matched the stripe on the foredeck to accentuate length. The rear seat hides a stowage area for fuel for the outboard motor.

Right: with seat removed, can is recessed in transom.

Plexiglas panels, that enclose the cab in bad weather, are housed in the partition between the interior and cockpit.

This 38x14ft hull has been restyled into a sedan cruiser with many automotive overtones. Large windows provide unprecedented visibility, and the cabin roof extends forward of the wind shield to reduce glare. The twin masts and overhead instrumentation were deemed distinctive innovations for that time.

the first 'cigarette' powerboats and propulsion systems. They shared a mutual appreciation for each other's talents and got on very well, so Bob Hobbs became part of the team and they created Exner-Hobbs Associates. Along with his new partner, Ex published a selection of his ideas in *Popular Boating* magazine, which received a great deal of positive attention. Using some of his contacts, Bob agreed to help Ex to get his foot in the door with some of the large boat-building firms. Because of the magazine

article, the task of soliciting some of the other companies became a much easier task. One of them was the newly formed marine division of Indiana Gearworks, Buehler Turbocraft. Directed by John Buehler, the company initially built 16ft long, inboard-powered jet boats that could run in just 3in of water. By 1962, the company had extended its range but wanted to go even further and develop fiberglass cabin cruisers. Buehler liked Ex's fresh designs and approached him about developing a complete line of fishing boats, sports runabouts and cruisers measuring up to 28ft. Ex set to work with Buehler's hull designer Dave Beech, and over the next twenty months came up with an exciting series of boats that would become Buehler's complete 1966 range. Exner, Inc even illustrated the Buehler sales brochure for the launch of the range at the 1966 Chicago Boat Show. Hobbs, Ex and Virgil Jr attended the show, welcome guests of the Buehler marketing team and made the most of the perfect publicity for the company.

It was also in 1962 that Ex joined forces with his son to set up their own design business, Virgil M Exner, Inc. Junior had just left the United States Air Force with the rank of Captain, and had already been carrying out freelance design work while still in service, becoming an accomplished stylist. He brought with him an on-going contract with Ghia, work he had been doing since 1955. The father and son team rented space from the architectural design company Lukenbach & Associates, and set up shop at 950 North Hunter Blvd, Birmingham, Michigan, just about a mile from home, employing a receptionist and modelers that moonlighted from Ford and Chrysler. Although Junior had little interest in powerboats at the beginning, he soon learned to appreciate their beauty and potential, and created many designs for the company.

On a visit to the New York Boat Show, Ex and Hobbs spoke with a Dutchman named Gerard Kouwenhoven. Kouwenhoven was the chief salesman on the Riva stand and its main distributor in Monaco. Riva was well-known for their classic wooden-hulled boats, but rumors in the industry said that Carlo Riva, head of the world famous boat manufacturer of Sarnico, was looking into building a large fiberglass cruiser. After discussing the project, Kouwenhoven asked Ex and Hobbs to design a super-luxury, semi-custom cruiser for the French and Italian Riviera, which differed from the

The exterior of the Cutty Sark *is shown here in a clay model at Exner's studio in Birmingham, Michigan.*

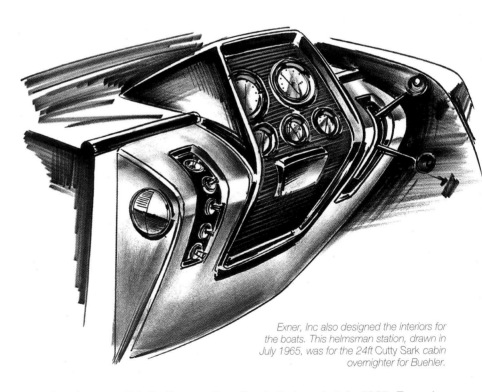

Exner, Inc also designed the interiors for the boats. This helmsman station, drawn in July 1965, was for the 24ft Cutty Sark *cabin overnighter for Buehler.*

CrisCraft currently selling in that market. In 1965, Ex and Virgil flew to Riva's headquarters in Sarnico, bringing with them their proposal for a 32ft cruiser. Riva got down on his hands and knees and spread the plans out all over his office floor. After going through the design with the

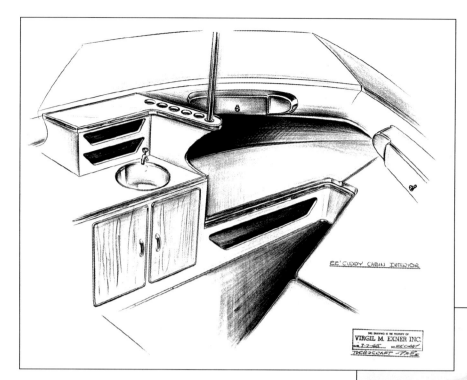

The interior proposal for the Cutty Sark.

26' CUDDY CABIN INTERIOR

THIS DRAWING IS THE PROPERTY OF
VIRGIL M. EXNER INC.
no. 7-2-65 no. 26' CABY
TURBOCRAFT - TREE

stylists, he got up and smiled. Much
to the relief of the Americans, Riva
beamed, "Yes! I like it, very much."
A verbal contract was made and
the designs were left with Riva, but
a few months later Virgil Jr found
himself in Italy, without his father,
working out a few teething problems
on a car being built for them by
Ghia. Whilst in the country, he took
the opportunity to meet up with
Hobbs and visit Carlo Riva to check
on progress. According to Virgil,
Hobbs became very argumentative
and aggressive when the discussion

*John Buehler obviously liked the Exner and Hobbs designs a great deal as
the resulting production models differ little from the initial designs. This is the
Cutty Sark, as advertised in Buehler's brochure for 1967.*

turned to costings and payment,
much to the embarrassment of the
young designer. Hobbs wanted
a royalty for each individual boat
produced, which was not standard
practice in the boat building industry.
Carlo took an instant dislike to Hobbs
and ended the meeting. Virgil phoned
his father and told him what had

*1966 Buehler 18ft Bolero. The Bolero was
a custom jet runabout that flaunted lean,
modern, youthful styling that, when added to
the deep V-shaped hull designed by William
Nielsen, gave a fast but comfortable ride.
This boat was selected by Popular Science
magazine as the 'Trend setter for '66' in its
February 1966 issue.*

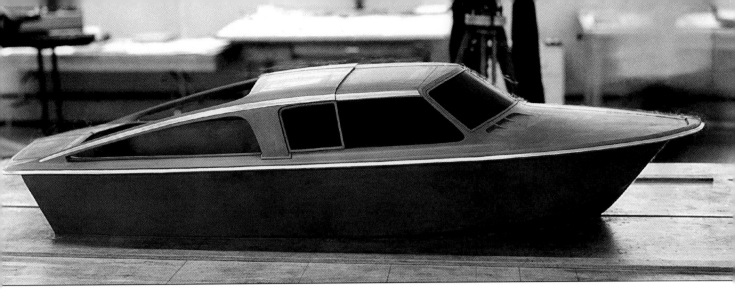

This 1966 clay model of the Bar Harbor featured a gullwing hard-top and fastback side rails to give an automotive feel to the sleek day cruiser.

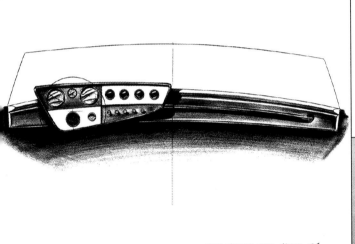

This sketch, drawn on 27th August 1965, shows a proposal for the planned Bar Harbor day cruiser control panel.

the right to the molds. He first bought a hull from Magnum and then two from Bertram. When, in 1969, he decided to sell the yard to the American Whittaker Corporation, the owners of Bertram, their hulls and designs were selected over Exner's and his design was shelved. Although Exner, Inc was paid for the consultation work, it never saw the realization of the beautiful craft. All was not lost, though, as this design led to further styling and consultancy

happened and on their return to the United States, the Exners and Hobbs parted company. Ex phoned Carlo in Italy. Had they lost the contract? No, not at all, but the boat-builder realized that his yard was not up to producing such a large cruiser as its first effort in fiberglass. He decided first to train his workforce and then start with an already ongoing production, buying

The Bar Harbor became one of Buehler's top sellers and was voted one of the top boats of 1966 by Boatcraft magazine.

The clay model seen here is for Buehler's 28ft Express Cruiser. Seen in the mirror is a ¼-scale model of a Duesenberg proposal, done by Virgil Jr.

contracts with other boat builders throughout the sixties, including Matthews, Brunswick, Pacemaker and Bristol, the largest of which was a 65ft cruiser for Pacemaker Boats of New Jersey.

In the studio, Virgil worked on the smaller boats while Ex liked styling the larger craft, both of them creating plans, detailed drawings and clay models as required. As most of the boat-makers had set hulls, the stylist's main task was to create detail changes on a predetermined superstructure, or create the superstructure from scratch, and they worked very closely with the bodyshop of the manufacturers, helping to overcome any technical difficulties. The pair came up with two sport runabouts for Brunswick, then helped with a 41ft Hatteras sport fishing cruiser in 1965 and a 44ft Mathews cabin cruiser in 1968.

While work continued with the cabin cruisers, the Exners kept close contact with Luigi Segre at Ghia. On 3rd April 1962, Ex and Segre signed an official contract for Exner, Inc to create two car designs each month through to the end of March 1963, including a ¼-scale clay model and sketches of instrument panels. More importantly, Segre and Sergio Coggiola flew to America on 25th January 1963, to visit with Ex and to discuss the possibility of opening a Ghia subsidiary in the United States. Segre had ambitions to become a series producer much like fellow Torinese coachbuilders Pininfarina and Bertone, and had already created the OSI

Buehler advertised the Express Cruiser in its 1967 brochure as being available in 24 or 28ft lengths with custom design. Exner's Jet Stream styling was a huge hit and transformed the way powerboats looked.

1965 Riva. Carlo Riva intended to make a series of fiberglass-hulled boats to complement his classic wooden-bodied powerboats. This was what Ex designed for him but it never saw production, as Riva sold his company to the American Whittaker Corporation, which it used its own design.

company. Opened in 1960, in conjunction with typewriter manufacturer Olivetti, Olivetti provided the finance and a factory building across the street from the Ghia coachworks, while Ghia supplied the personnel and skills. On 15th February 1963, after his return to Italy, Segre wrote to Ex saying that Ghia USA was no longer just a dream, but a necessity. He asked Ex to help with looking for a suitable location to buy or rent in Birmingham, and the possible set-up costs that he might incur. The plan was for Coggiola to have the US Ghia studio open by June of that year, with him doing the engineering and paperwork, Virgil Jr doing the designs, while initially at least, having the cars built in Turin. He also mentioned his visit to the Genoa Boat Show and was very interested in Ghia building Exner-designed powerboats, a completely new direction for the Italian company. He finished off by saying, "For your information, next Monday, I will go to hospital to undergo the operation I told you about and in some ten days everything will be over." Ex replied with a lengthy hand-written letter on 21st February but, tragically,

for Segre it was all over. He never lived to see the positive reply. The 44-year-old Italian died on Monday 28th February, following complications from a routine kidney operation. When Ex received the telegram from Ghia that same day saying that one of his closest friends had died, he was devastated. All plans for Ghia USA died along with Segre.

Powerboats were a large part of the Exner's business and leisure time, but they were also very aware of a sea change in the automobile market. The resurrection and restoration of classic names from car history was becoming big business, collectors throughout the world had started buying up old Rolls-Royce, Mercedes-Benz, Bugatti, and Duesenberg automobiles. In early 1963, *Esquire* magazine writer Diana Bartley contacted the Exners, asking where they thought car design was headed, and how did it relate to the latest fashion for older classics from the thirties. Expanding on this initial idea, our two illustrious stylists got down to designing what they thought some of those older cars would look like with contemporary bodywork.

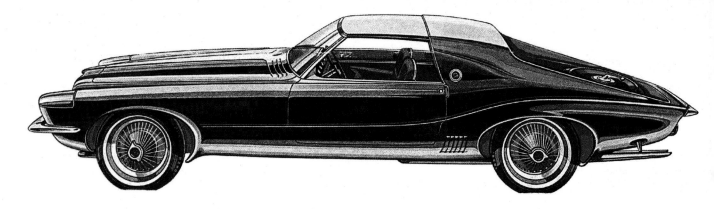

1963 Stutz Revival Car. The designs created by the Exners for the December 1963 Esquire *magazine were a breakthrough for Ex. No longer held back by corporate constraints, Ex created a series of drawings based on defunct automobile marques from the golden era of the 1920s and '30s, but with a modern interpretation. The Stutz Super Bearcat relied heavily on the 'Scott Fitzgerald era' Bearcat of the early twenties, including the Stutz radiator cowl and near horizontal spare wheel on the rear deck.*

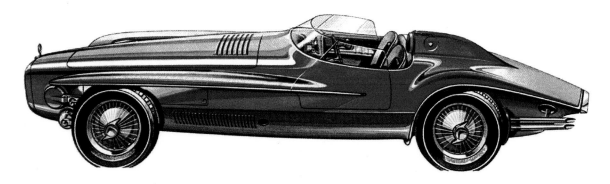

Mercer Revival Car. The Mercer for '64 was not an out-and-out race car like the raceabout it was based on, but more a lean, fast, comfortable road car. The long hood-short deck proportions were there, but the Mercer emphasized mechanical beauty with its large 17in, fully exposed wheels, and the racing-type gas filler cap mimicked original Mercer styling and complemented the open race car windshield.

This would prove to be the perfect vehicle for the classic long nose, short deck proportions that Ex had been trying to get into production for over a decade. In the December 1963 issue of *Esquire*, Exner published designs that would become known as the 'revival cars' and would once again pioneer styling that would spread across Detroit's design departments. Four neo-classic cars were shown: designs for Stutz, Duesenberg, Packard, and Mercer. Within that article, Exner explained, "What we are trying to do is capture the spirit of the older car design and body in a modern package. We believe not only that greater stress should be put on the development and continuous refinement of a distinctive character for each marque, but also that the market for luxury cars can be greatly stimulated by some real effort to recapture some of the elegance and originality, which make many of the old cars so interesting and exciting to us yet today. And even within the present economic limitations, an interesting number of original body types, each with an individual character and purpose, is still feasible."

The Stutz Super Bearcat was based around the 2-seat convertible roadster of the same name from 1933 but featured a sliding canopy instead of the old fabric one and had an integrated roll bar built into the rear quarter-panel. Styling cues for this, as with the other three, were well known to admirers of Exner's work; a classic front grille, open wheelarches, wire wheels and trunk-mounted spare all typified the elegant days of a bygone era. The dark blue color was complimented with red and cream pinstriping. As for the Duesy, this manifested itself as a 4-door phaeton, even down to the twin cowls and two windscreens but wore a lower, sleeker body with clamshell front fenders reminiscent of the ill-fated Norseman; these fenders held trick headlamps which folded up neatly into the nose of the fender. All of the revival cars rolled on large 16 or 17in diameter wheels, not industry standard sizes at that time, but it helped with dimensions and proportions for the cars. The Packard was the weakest link here, based on a 1934 Twin Six Convertible Victoria. To achieve a

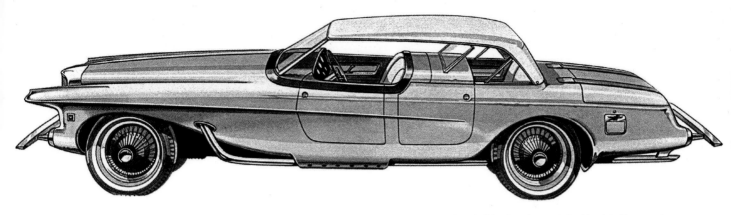

Duesenberg Revival Car. The more formal Duesenberg appeared as a Sport Phaeton and wore clamshell fenders that stretched back to the rear doors, and held trick headlights that folded up into the nose of the front surface. This drawing and the other Revival Cars seen in Esquire were all done by Ex and Virgil Jr.

Packard Revival Car. Of the Revival Cars, as they came to be known, Ex said, "We propose to show what each of them might be offering for 1964, assuming either that each manufacturer had pursued a policy of refinement and modernisation of his cars' identifying characteristics, or that each had decided to resume business after a thirty-year lapse." With the Packard, the design didn't quite work as a whole, although parts of it were inspirational. A fabric-covered, folding metal roof hid rear passengers from prying eyes but paid the price in limited rear observation. Ex managed to get his free-standing headlights on the Packard, although they flipped down into the front grille area when not in use.

coach shape, Ex had to go against one of his own styling rules and enclose the rear wheelarch. The Packard did offer privacy to rear passengers as planned, but at the cost of side and rear visibility. At the front were flip headlights set either side of a nicely executed Packard grille, but overall, this design didn't quite gel. The design that did work incredibly well, though, was the last one – the Mercer. Perhaps because of its racing lines, Exner enjoyed working on this version of the 1911 Raceabout and it quite clearly shows styling from yet another Chrysler show car – the Valiant-based XNR. The 1964 Mercer was not a race car but, as Ex described it, a big, fast, comfortable road car, a lean, powerful machine with emphasis on mechanical beauty. But it was all there: the low sports windscreen, asymmetrical hump behind the drivers head, racing-style gas filler cap on the right rear wing and sculpted front and rear fenders. Simply beautiful.

The positive feedback from these led to three

more great names from automobile history receiving an update: Bugatti, Pierce-Arrow, and a Jordan Playboy. Little came of most of these cars but the article was extremely influential, with both the public and designers alike, and of the seven, three got as far as being built as working prototypes and one, the Stutz, went into production. Virgil Jr remembers: "There was a bit of a movement going on to get back into classic looking cars and my father had started to get back into the long hood, short deck proportions for those '62 models, and he was pushing for the industry to go in that direction. Of course, these cars were around when he was growing up; especially the Duesenberg was his favorite."

Children of the mid-sixties would see all of these cars recreated in their own homes when the toy manufacturer Renwal bought the rights to these cars and released its 'Revival Series' in 1965 and 1966 based on Exner's designs. Exner, Inc worked closely with the toy maker to

The front cover of the October 1964 issue of men's magazine, True, featured four more Exner designs, although oddly, none was mentioned inside.

THE MAN'S MAGAZINE

50 CENTS OCTOBER 1964 A FAWCETT PUBLICATION

TRUE

WHAT'S NEW IN THE 1965 CARS

RITUAL 'CUTTING' BY THE KU KLUX KLAN
A SHOCKER BY WILLIAM BRADFORD HUIE

THE SHARPSHOOTER THE RUSSIANS FEAR MOST
OLYMPIC PREVIEW BY DALE SHAW

A GIRL FOR YOUR BED, A MAN FOR YOUR FIELDS
SLAVERY TODAY BY JOHN KEATS

develop the drawings and ⅛-scale clay models ready for production of ¹⁄₂₅-scale plastic model kits. Virgil spent a lot of time at the Renwal factory in Mineola, New York, looking over different kits that could offer individual pieces to be used on the cars, saving on expensive retooling where possible. The whole series was very popular and once the real cars had been built, they were shown alongside the models on the Renwal stand at the big Chicago Toy Fair. The first year Renwal used the Mercer and the following year it exhibited the Bugatti. And it was towards real cars that Ex was directing his efforts. Shortly after the publication of the *Esquire* feature, he was approached by the Copper Development Association of New York. It was planning to produce a concept vehicle made predominantly with copper, bronze, and brass

components as an advertising tool aimed at the automotive industry. After seeing the *Esquire* article and talking with Ex, the association chose his Mercer design to carry its flag. At this time, Ghia was struggling financially and was unable to pay its consultants, the Exner-Ghia contract had been suspended, and the sheet-metal genius Sibona had just left to go into partnership with the Bassano Brothers, also in Turin. Friend and fellow industrial designer Brook Stevens recommended that Exner, Inc should have the prototype car built by the new company. It had just finished creating his Studebaker Sceptre and he had been very pleased with the outcome. Being aware of Sibona's talents, and on Brooks' recommendation, Sibona-Bassano built the Mercer on a specially lengthened (by 15in) Shelby Cobra chassis. The car debuted in December 1964 as the Mercer Cobra and featured unique swing-out headlights, bumpers, grille, exhaust protector, and wheel covers, along with many other trim items, that received a covering from copper alloys. Mechanically, copper disc brakes, copper alloy brake lines, radiator tanks, copper instrument cases, and a Ford Cobra 259in³ engine adorned with brass ancillaries, all helped to brighten the engine bay and body. The Copper Development Association showed this graceful and elegant car for nearly a decade before selling it for an impressive $165,000. It is now thought to be part of Gen William Lyon's automobile collection.

Opposite: 1964 Mercer Cobra. Built on a lengthened Ford Cobra chassis by Italian Carozzeria Sibona-Bassano, the car was powered by a Cobra 259ci engine and featured unique swing out headlights, bumpers, grille, exhaust protector, and wheel covers, along with many other trim items made from copper alloys. The Copper Development Association showed this graceful and elegant car for nearly a decade before selling it to a private collector. (Blackhawk Collection)

1964 Mercer Cobra. Shortly after Ex revealed his thoughts on contemporary designs for classic cars in Esquire magazine, he was contacted by the Copper Development Company, which wanted a show car that would project the more positive aspects of using brass and copper alloys within the automobile industry. After discussing the idea with Ex, it commissioned him to design and build a car based on his Mercer sportscar. This was Exner's finished design and, when created in metal, went virtually unchanged. (From the collections of The Henry Ford)

In 1964, Ex had the unusual opportunity of buying a piece of motoring history when the editor of *Automobile Quarterly* told him he knew the whereabouts of the very last Bugatti chassis ever built. At the cessation of hostilities in 1945, Ettore Bugatti planned all-new road and racing cars in order to restart the company after it was destroyed through bombing during World War II. Unfortunately, he died in August 1947, but Ettore's son, Roland, took up the mantle to produce the mid-engined Type 251 race car and the luxury Type 101 convertible. Based on a modified Type 57 chassis, the 101s were powered by the same 3.3-litre straight-eight engine as the legendary Type 57s, with the supercharged 101C (C standing for Compresseur) versions boosting power to 200bhp. The Type 251 race car failed to perform to expectations, and the company's attempts at automobile production were halted. As a result, between 1951 and 1956, when production ceased, only six complete Type 101s were built, five convertibles and one coupe, and one car without a body, which lay forgotten at the Bugatti factory until American Allen Henderson found it and bought it from the Bugatti estate in 1961.

By 1964, Henderson was suffering ill health and told a friend, L Scott Bailey, owner of *Automobile Quarterly* magazine, that he wanted to sell some of his collection. Bailey knew Ex and, while at the launch party for the Duesenberg at the Exner, Inc studios, he mentioned that Henderson was going to part with some of his Bugattis, including the last chassis built. Both Exners were

very interested and, in January 1965, they went to New York for a meeting with Bailey to discuss the Bugatti. He took them to lunch at former Bugatti racing driver Rene Dryfuss' La Chanteclaire restaurant on East 49th Street, where they were joined by industrial designer and friend, Brook (Kip) Stevens. Over the meal, the group talked

1965 Bugatti model. A detailed half clay model was produced and set against a mirror to give the impression of a complete car. The model still exists and is owned by Virgil Exner Jr. (Peter Madle)

1965 Bugatti 101CX. This white on black negative sketch was Exner's proposal for a Bugatti, to be built on the last Bugatti chassis ever made. (Peter Madle)

Although Luigi Segre was now dead, Ex still had close links with Ghia and Karmann in Germany, and was asked directly by Wilhelm Karmann Jr to develop the original Volkswagen Karmann Ghia. This is one of two Exner proposals for a new 1500 coupe, drawn in 1965.

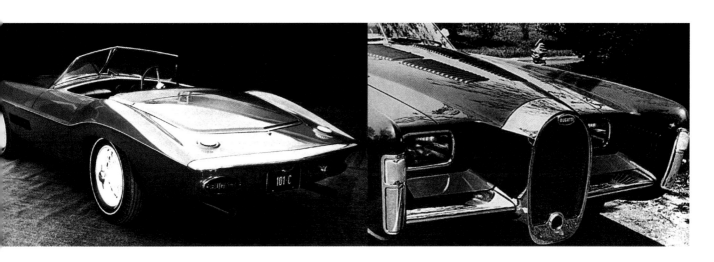

The finished Bugatti was produced once again by Ghia of Turin. The rear end treatment was much better looking than the heavy front view.

143

Exner's planned revival of the Duesenberg marque started in robust fashion and, when the prototype was launched, it made news around the world. The January 1966 edition of Popular Mechanics magazine had the car on its front cover and gave a glowing three-page report on the planned release of the production model.

POPULAR MECHANICS

JAN. 1966
35 CENTS

'66 DUESENBERG

7 big cars
rich people drive!

3 racing engines
for your car!

SNOWMOBILES
Hottest cold-weather sport!

BUILD 'TEACUP'
The boat that teaches you to sail!

Duesenberg

month later, Junior, along with his best friend, Mike Cleary, collected the chassis and trailered it through winter blizzards back to Birmingham, towed by the '64 Plymouth wagon. One month after that, Junior returned to Perth Amboy and bought Henderson's Galibier bodied Type 57 for just $1500, driving it all the way home.

Ex and Junior immediately started work on producing a Revival Car design for the Bugatti, reminiscent of the French classics made by Ettore. Based around the traditional Bugatti grille, Ex envisioned a low-slung, muscular roadster body that swept back into a curved Corvette like rear end. As with many clays built within the industry, a small, half-model was made, then set against a mirror, to give the impression of a complete car. Highly detailed and finished in dark blue, the model is still owned by Virgil Jr. Ex got expert help with engineering the car from close friends Paul Farago and Dale Cosper, who assisted with detailed plans and the ⅛th clay model. Ghia still owed Exner, Inc over $27,000 in unpaid design consultancy fees, so an agreement was come to whereby Ghia would build a full-size body for the chassis,

about what could be done with the chassis and a visit to its location in New Jersey was organized. When Ex and Junior arrived at Henderson's house in Perth Amboy, NJ, they found a rundown house and a large barn. They were shown around by the housekeeper, who, on opening the barn doors, revealed a line of fourteen unrestored Bugattis including a Type 57 SC Corsica roadster, a 1939 Type 57 four-door Galibier sedan, and the chassis. The Type 101 chassis, numbered 101506, was fitted with a supercharged engine and a basic box seat, so that it could be driven. Through Scott Bailey, Ex purchased the naked car from Henderson for the sum of $2500, and a

for free, including the cost of shipping both ways and the debt would be considered paid in full. The chassis was shortened 18in to make a 112in wheelbase by Virgil Jr and Mike Cleary before it was shipped to Ghia, along with the full-length prop shaft, which Ghia modified. The rest of the right-hand drive mechanics and the super-charged 3.3-litre straight-eight stayed original. Minor changes to the initial sketches and model were made; traditionally routed exhaust pipes were fitted instead of exterior ones, the raked back one-piece windshield changed into a two-piece V shape, and the front side and indicator lights were integrated into the front fenders. As with the model built by and for the Exners, the real Bugatti wore dark blue paint and wire wheels with spinner caps. In a brave attempt to revive the marque, Ex displayed the Bugatti 101C-X at the 1965 Turin Auto Salon to much interest and acclaim, but he failed to obtain major financing for a production series so, once again, he had to shelve the plans. He did keep the car for many years, putting a thousand miles on the clock before selling it to Thomas Barett III in 1969. The car still survives and is also owned by General William Lyons.

The Exners did not give up hope of seeing one of their Revival Cars go into limited production, and came very close with their next attempt, the 1966 Duesenberg. Fritz Duesenberg, son of August Duesenberg, along

with promoter Mylo Record, were very interested in resurrecting the classic name and had already made one unsuccessful attempt in the fifties, using a Packard as a donor. Fritz gave Ex and Junior a positive reception when they met in January 1964. Throughout the year,

1966 Duesenberg. This picture of the planned Duesenberg was taken from the now highly sought-after brochure that was released in 1966. The car took very little from Exner's initial proposal for Duesenberg, first seen in the 1963 Esquire magazine article, and more resembled the Stutz.

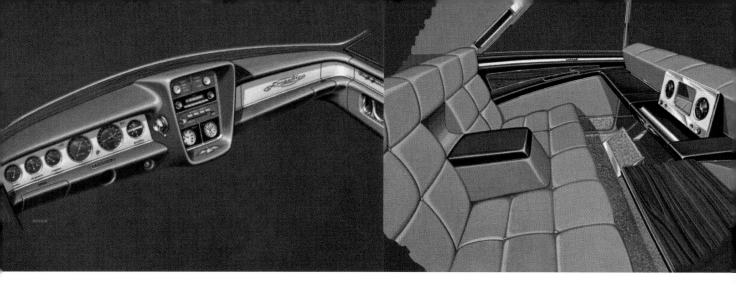

The planned Duesenberg D came with a sumptuous interior, developed by Exner, Inc, and was made with the finest materials available. A host of convenience options included individual reading lights, air conditioning, carpeted foot rests, television, vanity mirror for rear passengers, and a bar.

Ex had many meetings with the Duesenberg Corporation team, supplying preliminary sketches, and scale models of a suggested prototype. On the 1st September 1964, he signed a two-year contract with them to develop a design for production. Over the next three months, Ex and Junior prepared no less than fourteen different exterior designs and three fully-detailed ¼-scale clay models for a Duesenberg sedan. On 23rd December, Fred and Ex selected the final design from the three models, allowing Ex to start creating scale drafts.

Cliff Voss joined Exner, Inc for one year in 1965, and worked with Paul Farago and Dale Cosper in assisting the Exners to engineer a vehicle that would be capable of limited production. This time around, it was based on Chrysler Imperial running gear, something the Exners and Ghia felt comfortable with. At that time, Ghia had just finished building the last ten Crown Imperial limousines for the 1965 model year and had not yet sold the limousine tooling to Barrieros in Spain, so it was no trouble to set the prototype Duesy on a stretched Imperial convertible chassis as they had done for the limos. Farago was sent to live in Turin to act as resident Duesenberg Chief Engineer and to supervise the construction by Ghia. By February 1965, Ex and Junior had completed their task and had sent all the details to Farago. The Italians worked hard to produce a full-size plaster manikin and in June they were joined for six weeks by Ex, refining the final 'master' model. He returned to Italy again in November 1965, to oversee the mock-up of the interior and to check on the progress of the metal body that was by then under construction. Exner's design differed greatly from his *Esquire* magazine Duesenberg; the version for 1966 still featured clamshell fenders but the phaeton had been replaced by a classy four-door sedan. Although measuring over 20ft in length, the new Duesy was beautifully proportioned. Jim Dunne from *Popular Mechanics* summed it up in his article in January 1966: "There is one obvious drawback to having body styling that is as balanced as that of the new Duesenberg. Big as the car is, its massiveness does not show up readily, because the lines are so well proportioned ... Destined to be a classic as soon as it is born." And massive it was, the hood alone stretched 82in and peaked with the much-copied Duesenberg grille. Ex and Junior produced three different clay model designs before agreeing on the final recipe. The wheelbase was shortened to 137.5in and the all-steel body measured 80.32in wide, giving the car a dramatic presence on the road. The 5700lb of luxury were powered by a Chrysler 440in^3 V8 that would have put out 425hp in the production models, although the prototype utilized a stock 350hp version.

All of this power was transferred into a three-speed Torqueflite automatic gearbox and tempered by disc-brakes all round. The designers wanted to use large 16 or 17in wheels to help proportion the car, but in 1965 these were not industry standard sizes so they enrolled the skills of Firestone to create special tall 15in tires that had two 1in white-wall lines, the first near the center and another just below the tread, giving the specially made Dayton wire wheels the illusion of being 17in wheels. The rear suicide doors opened to reveal an opulent but formal interior of cashmere and leather, and utilized many Imperial parts. The development and construction of the new Duesenberg is estimated to have cost $60,000. Exner's designs had been freely shown in the motoring press and even before the prototype had been completed, general sales manager Bryan A Orr had received many letters of interest. On 10th May 1965 he sent a letter to everyone that had shown an interest in purchasing a new Duesy. The car would be available in 1966 at a cost of $19,500.

Exner with Duesenberg. Once again built by Ghia, the finished car was all that Ex had hoped it would be. Orders were taken from some of the most influential people in America, including Elvis Presley and Frank Sinatra. Unfortunately, one of the major financial partners backed out and the project stumbled. The prototype car was seized and sold off to pay outstanding debts, and is now part of the Bortz Collection.

Compared to $6600 for an Imperial LeBaron, it was clear to see that this was a car intended purely for the seriously rich. A deposit of $5000 was requested for the recipient to be placed on the waiting list. This was followed with a letter from the Chairman of the Duesenberg board of directors, Fred Duesenberg, on 25th August. Deposits were received from fifty people, the first from Philip Knight Wrigley of the chewing gum family, followed by celebrities like Elvis Presley and Jerry Lewis.

On the morning of 29th March 1966, the Duesenberg had its premiere in the Cole Porter Ballroom of the Sheraton-Lincoln Hotel, Indianapolis, to invited guests. Fred and Fritz Duesenberg attended the two-day launch while Bryan Orr received more deposits. By this stage, a factory had been sourced in Italy to build the bodies and another in Indianapolis to marry the custom coachwork to the chassis. Work was started in both locations to equip the sites for the venture. The Duesenbergs hoped to be build fifty cars in the first year, increasing to two hundred the next, reaching a steady five hundred thereafter. Yearly styling changes were to be minimal, although a convertible and a limousine were planned for 1967. The car made its public debut at the 1966 Indy 500 race where it was parked on a display stand, and received huge amounts of attention. The car was then transported to Detroit for a private showing at the Exner Studio. One hundred top automotive executives and members of the local press were invited to the showing and reception. When word got around, they actually had nearly three hundred guests arrive including key design managers from Ford, Chrysler, and General Motors. If all of this sounds too good to be true, well, it was. Almost at the eleventh hour, Fred J McManis Jr, a major financer of the project, pulled out,

leaving the Duesenbergs struggling to find money. Lacking enough funds of their own, and failing to find backers, the operation fell apart. Financially, this was a major blow to the Exners, over this period of time neither of the designers paid themselves wages, earning enough money to pay the rent on the building and little else. For Ex, however, the collapse of the project meant so much more. Given the passion that he had had since early childhood for the Duesenberg, and the fact that his dream of seeing his own version of the marque back on the highways was completely sunk, Exner was crushed. In order to pay off debts owed by the Duesenberg Corporation, the prototype car was seized and sold, and now resides in the Auburn-Cord-Duesenberg Museum.

The car did have a major influence on some makers, especially Ford. Henry Ford II was one of the visitors to the Exner studio and adored it, so it was no surprise when the Continental Mk III arrived in 1969 looking very much like a 1966 Duesenberg, but it wasn't just Ford. Ex's neo-classic look came to dominate Detroit in the seventies, with almost every full-size car featuring a long hood/short deck and sporting formal grilles, opera windows, trunk straps, landau bars and sculpted fenders, including Cadillac's Eldorado and Chrysler's Imperial. With little regular work coming in to keep two stylists busy, it was decided that Junior would have to leave the business and find employment with one of the big manufacturers in Detroit. In 1967, he started at Ford, leaving Ex to run the business.

To replace his son, Ex took on a young artist to help out. Dave Reid had just left school and would stay with Ex until 1969 when he followed Junior to Ford. It wasn't all doom and gloom for Exner, Inc though. Out of the ashes of the Duesenberg project came the hope of yet another

1968 Stutz Blackhawk boat-tail coupe. This was one of many early proposals for a Stutz. Although this design got no further than the drawing board, Ex returned to this style when asked to create a Stutz powerboat. (From the collections of The Henry Ford)

opportunity to build a limited production luxury car. The phoenix came in the form of an American investment banker from New York named James O'Donnell.

O'Donnell and Exner had first met in 1966 when Ex was trying to obtain financing for the Duesenberg. He had gone to Wall Street to ask for financial and management help. He approached O'Donnell and showed him the prototype, which was awaiting the capital for production. O'Donnell was bowled over by the car, but after thorough investigation, including a fact-finding trip to Italy, he concluded that the project was not well-planned and in serious debt, so he declined the invitation to invest. However, the fascination with the classic car had taken hold of his imagination. A few months later he contacted Ex, wanting to explore the possibility of manufacturing a different luxury car based around the Duesenberg design.

In August 1968, O'Donnell visited the Exner studio to discuss the project. In a resume of his Stutz experience written in 1991, O'Donnell remembers: "He had many dream cars but one was outstanding. It resembled a Batmobile but was not threatening looking. Mr Exner pointed out that the front of the car had a phallic look which created unconscious excitement. Whatever the reason, it looked like a winner. Not being a professional car maker, I asked Mr Exner if we could get another opinion on our design from an expert in the field. Mr Exner had expressed the belief that we should go with General Motors and their long-hooded front for the chassis. The Pontiac Grand Prix was his choice. At that time, John Z De Lorean headed the Pontiac Division at General Motors

and he agreed to meet with us and give us his opinion on our project. Mr De Lorean was a very tall and handsome man with a sense of humor and no nonsense approach, I liked him. After a few hours of discussion he concluded that our project was feasible, our choice of the car was correct, and if we wanted to go ahead with the Pontiac Grand Prix he would give us all the cooperation we needed." The charismatic engineer not only agreed that GM would be able to supply bodiless Pontiacs should the car go as far as production, but also that at a reasonable cost, of course, the new car could be serviced at any GM dealer, unlike other exotic vehicles on the market that required specialized and expensive workshop facilities. The use of a domestic chassis meant that the company would only have to manufacture and mount the body then fit the interior. The engine, brakes, steering, electrics, and the rest would be pre-assembled by Pontiac. Now the pair had a firm footing to set off on, what they needed was a name.

The original Stutz Motor Company had by this time, been dormant for thirty years and the name had become public domain. O'Donnell was an admirer of those classics from the late-1920s and suggested it to Ex, not realizing that Ex had, along with Duesenberg, been a lifelong enthusiast of the marque and had even sketched a body

Opposite: The Stutz had no options, as none were required. The car came with every conceivable amenity, including electric seats, windows, and door looks, along with tinted windows and air conditioning. This picture of the Stutz prototype was taken at Graceland in Memphis at a Stutz gathering in 2006. (Peter Madle)

This photo of the rear three quarter view of the prototype Stutz sitting in its body buck, was taken at the factory at Cavallermaggiore, near Turin. (From the collections of The Henry Ford)

The Stutz Blackhawk prototype two-door hard-top was completed by December 1969 by Ghia artisans at a reputed cost of $300,000 and made its New York debut in January 1970. From left to right are Paul Farago, unknown model, Ex and James O'Donnell. (From the collections of The Henry Ford)

proposal as a youngster, so this suggestion was well-received. With this agreement made, O'Donnell eventually raised $1,200,000 in funds and incorporated Stutz Motor Cars of America. The founders would receive one-third of the company for minimal cash outlay but maximum donation of time and skill to the corporation, without pay. Each founder received his allotment according to his promised participation and talents. Private investors would buy one-third of the company at a price substantially lower than the price of the stock to be offered to the public at a future date. As a founder, Ex became a director of the company and created a revised design for a Stutz, intentionally incorporating many of the features intended for the 1966 Duesenberg. Plans and clays were made for a coupe and a five-passenger sedan limousine, both to be built around Pontiac rolling stock. O'Donnell wished to build a convertible named the Bearcat, but government legislation at that time made it almost impossible, so the first Stutz was planned as a coupe. On 1st October 1968, O'Donnell purchased the very first Pontiac Grand Prix from Audette Pontiac, Inc from Troy, Mi, paying $4389. The 1969 model was then delivered to Creative Industries, a high-tech model making shop in Detroit. There, Ex fashioned a clay model of the new Stutz according to the vital measurement of the Grand Prix. It was crucial that the new Stutz body met every dimension of the donor car. When finished, the clay model had the exact look of the proposed car, and, when he was satisfied, 'skins', or plastic forms, were molded over the clay sculpture. The skins were then used to create a wooden mannequin over which steel body parts could be hammered into body-panels. The body parts would then be placed in a large fixture where a Grand Prix chassis awaited the welding process. The mannequin was finally finished in July 1969 with the prototype two-door hard-top completed in December by Ghia artisans at a reputed cost of $300,000. It fitted perfectly to the Pontiac chassis.

While the prototype was under development, O'Donnell made many trips to Italy looking for a manufacturing site and small parts suppliers. The site chosen was in Cavallermaggiore, near Turin. Facilities and skilled workers were available, and it was a desirable site from cost of living and transportation points of view. Paul Farago and Dale Cosper helped Sergio Coggiola from Ghia to set up Carozzeria Saturn, a company created purely to build the cars using skilled locals. They also applied pressure to Ex to try and get him to simplify some of the extreme styling and curves that needed to be created at the factory. Initially, Ex wouldn't budge from his design stance but in the end he capitulated and revised the rear end of the car.

The Stutz Blackhawk prototype was flown to New York City and made its debut in the Basildon Room of the Waldorf-Astoria Hotel on 26th January 1970. The car was a hit with the American and international press alike. The launching of the most expensive American-built production car in history attracted interest from Associated Press, Reuters, *The New York Times*, and other newspapers, along with three New York television stations, magazines and foreign and domestic radio stations. With a base price of $22,500 for the coupe, up to a staggering $75,000 for the proposed VIP parade phaeton, the new Stutz was marketed at the super-rich of the world. In his launch speech, O'Donnell announced that Stutz planned to release a convertible as soon as was practicable, a road-going Indy 500 type race car, and a limousine. Delivery was expected four months after the initial order was placed and only one hundred cars would be built in the first year of production, rising to five hundred thereafter; exclusivity was guaranteed. Time would show that production never reached anywhere near those numbers and the car became even more sought-after because of it.

People that had shown an interest in the Duesenberg were contacted along with others that had seen the Stutz in the media. The list of celebrities and royalty that bought a Stutz is long and impressive, but the most famous client had to be 'The King', Elvis Presley. Elvis bought Stutz #2 from California Stutz distributor Jules Meyers. There are a number of stories about how Elvis acquired the first production car, most focusing on how he beat Frank Sinatra to a dealership and paid for the car with cash, but a recent interview with Mr Meyers sheds light on the story. Elvis had phoned Meyers asking to see the car, so an appointment was made and he drove the Blackhawk to Hillcrest, Elvis' California home when he was filming his movies. When Elvis saw the car, he wanted it immediately, without the four-month wait. Meyers explained that this was only the second one built and his only demonstrator, but Elvis argued that Stutz would sell more cars if people saw him driving around in a Stutz rather than Meyers. You can't fault the logic there, but Meyers explained that he needed the car a few days later to exhibit at a show. The singer had not endorsed a product since 1954 but agreed to let Meyers have it back for the show and allowed some publicity photos to be taken with him and the car. The deal was done and Meyers got a lift home. Elvis would go on to buy three more cars from Stutz, with two still on show at Graceland, and it would become the only car he would drive on his own. The last picture of Elvis taken before his death in 1977 was of the singer driving through the gates of his home in Memphis behind the wheel his latest Stutz.

From 1968 through 1988, the Stutz was sold around the world, with production averaging around fifty units per year. Models included coupes, convertibles, four-door sedans, bulletproof limousines, and forty-six special

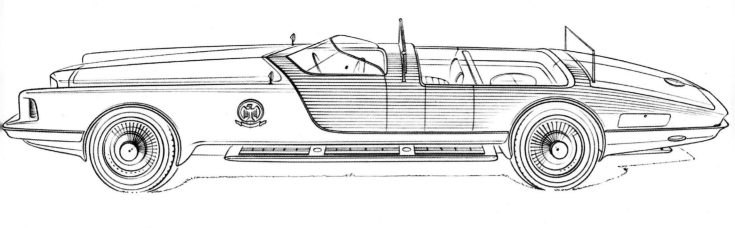

PRELIMINARY STUDY / VIRGIL M. EXNER INC. JULY '66

On 28th December 1966, the Detroit News reported that Ex had been retained to create the most spectacular circus ever made. With a bill that was expected to exceed $250,000, entrepreneur Paul W Lang of New York, intended to take the European style show to London and open by May 1970. This massive VIP parade phaeton would have stretched 25ft long and 7ft wide, and was intended to carry Lang and two tame lions.

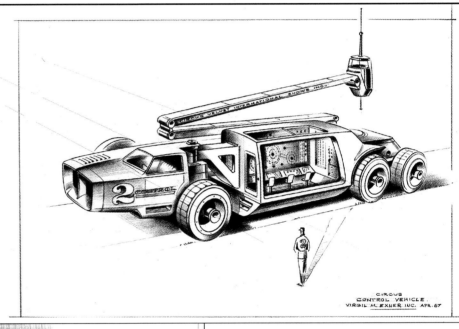

CIRCUS
CONTROL VEHICLE.
VIRGIL M. EXNER INC. APR. 67

Above & left: As the train rolled into town, it would disgorge a fleet of vehicles that would parade through the main street. With plans to open shows in Mexico and Europe, Lang requested designs for lighting vehicles, animal transportation, and trucks that would automatically erect the huge big top. By April 1967, Ex had created many of the vehicles, including a Control Vehicle, seen here in a preliminary sketch and developed into a color illustration.

four-door convertible military sedans for the Royal Guard of King Fahd of Saudi Arabia and King Hassan of Morocco. Paolo Martin, who also designed the Royale and Diplomatica, carried out later styling updates based on Exner styling cues. One of the most fascinating areas of this

Ex and Lang were interviewed by the Detroit News. Lang was quoted as saying, "I think Exner's the best there is." Exner, however, was reported as being a little stunned by the whole thing, and said, "Nobody's ever done anything like this before." But his bubbling enthusiasm overcame his obvious disbelief. Ex created the big top to complement the vehicles. If the project had progressed further, Ex would also have designed the train and railway carriages.

period was the proposed Stutz VIP mentioned at the launch in 1969. This idea and design stemmed from a project that Ex had just finished.

In 1966, he had been contacted by a businessman named Paul W Lang. The forty-six-year-old telephoned Ex from New York, explaining that he was a self-made

Seen here with Dow Chemical markings, this truck was actually another vehicle from the Velvet Circus fleet. Ex had connections with Dow because he produced a unique 1/4-scale clay model car, which it used for advertising for many years. The hope was that Dow would sponsor the vehicle. Going against what one might expect from a Barnum-type endeavor, Lang was very reclusive, and ultimately, unstable. His son phoned Ex and told him to drop the project completely.

man, making his money developing light-equipment, and cameras for the movie industry in Hollywood. Now semi-retired, he wanted to fulfil his lifetime dream of creating a circus that was bigger, better and more exciting than anything that had gone before. His plan was to have a specially constructed circus-train of over 100 cars that would roll into a town or city and disgorge a collection of unique circus vehicles that could parade through the town and then help erect a big top. Lang envisioned a 14,000-seat amphitheatre that would show a cast of 1000 performers, and be automated to the point that few riggers or roustabouts would be required. His wish list included light-trucks, tent-trucks, cars for the artists, all the animals, and a parade car for the director. The cost of the vehicles alone was expected to be $250,000.

The idea appealed to and fascinated Exner so he started the project straight away. With the help of close friend and ex-Chrysler colleague Maury Baldwin, they had a design for many of the vehicles for the Velvet Circus as it was known, done within a matter of weeks. Beautifully designed vehicles and even a big top tent were delicately liveried. Individual vehicles started to progress from drawing board to the clay model stage when Ex received another call from Lang, but this was Richard Lang, Paul's son. Ex was informed that due to mental illness, Richard was looking after his father's estate and was not prepared to give funding for something he thought of as a pipe dream and instructed Ex to cancel the project. Sadly the Velvet Circus was shelved after much work had already been completed, with Exner receiving no money for all his

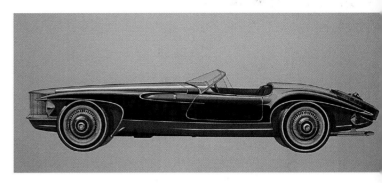

James O'Donnell saw Exner's proposal for the Circus Parade Car and wanted to turn it into a Stutz. Time would show that it only got as far as this proposal. (Peter Madle)

Yet another contract that Exner, Inc acquired was the job of creating a ¼-scale advanced design car for Dow Chemicals, based in Midland. MI. This photo, taken at Creative Industries in Detroit, is the completed and DiNoc-covered model, which the chemical company used for advertising.

This is one of two Mercedes 230 SL proposals that were done for Sergio Peninfarina in 1966 and 1967 when Exner, Inc entered into a short contract with the Italian design house. Neither designs was developed further.

effort. Hope shone briefly on one of the planned vehicles when James O'Donnell later saw the sketch of the Director's parade phaeton. This would be the Stutz VIP, to be produced in very small numbers at a cost of $75,000. Alas, this was also not to be, as Stutz concentrated on selling the coupe and convertible version, no orders were taken for the car, and no time was dedicated to develop the idea, so the sketch remained just that.

Throughout the late sixties and into the seventies Ex continued to do consultancy work for Ghia, Pininfarina, and Karmann, but with the stress and work that Ex was putting into the Stutz project too, it was no surprise that he ended up in hospital once again in October 1969, complaining of stomach pains. He spent five days in hospital while tests were undertaken. He was joined in his room by Chrysler stylist Dave Cummins: "When I arrived at the hospital, I was asked if I would like to share a room with another 'car guy', to which I said yes. Imagine my surprise when I realized it was Virgil Exner. My admiration for his work was the reason that I joined Chrysler. He had been there for a short time for diagnosis of some internal problem. He kept saying 'my guts ache!' which prevented rest or any sleep. He would often, at 2:00am say, 'Dave, are you awake?' to which my response would be 'I am now', and we would converse until after sunrise. We talked over many things and I asked him why he wanted to work for Chrysler in the first place. 'I wanted,' he said, 'to bring a professional design organization to the last of the Big Three.'" He certainly did that.

After tests were carried out, it was found that Ex had severe heart disease and underwent further by-pass surgery.

Virgil's health problems were exacerbated when he started smoking again in 1969, much to the annoyance of the family. Marie Exner told me that when Junior found out that his father had started smoking again while they were sitting around the dining table for a family meal, he almost jumped up and bopped his father on the nose. Junior was still a heavy smoker himself at that time, but the whole family was aware of the danger Ex was putting himself in. In 1970, he closed the

Ballerina in dressing room. Pastel. 1957.
(From the collections of The Henry Ford)

Snow in the Alps. Watercolor. 1958.

French village. Watercolor. 1959.

offices at 940 South Hunter Blvd, Birmingham and continued working from his studio at home. This move allowed him time to concentrate on more of the fine art work that he had started at the time of his heart attack in 1956. Ex had found plans for European castles and had been envisioning how they would look if they had not been ruined, recreating them in pastels, watercolors, and oils. His artistic talent knew few boundaries and he successfully drew landscapes, still life, and portraits with equal ease. Automotive and power boat work did not stop. In 1972, the Stutz Blackhawk received a face-lift which included a one-piece windscreen, a second side window and a more traditional rear bumper that enclosed the trashcan lid spare wheel. Work was done on modifying the Duesenberg design from 1966 to create the Stutz

Bearcat roadster, but it would not be built until 1979, six years after Exner's death. His personal transportation was a 1971 Blackhawk, painted in black with a red interior, of course, although in late 1972, on the advice of friend and neighbor Bill Mitchell, VP of GM Styling, Ex purchased a light metallic green 1973 Oldsmobile 98 four-door sedan as a family car. Through 1972 and into the following year, Ex worked on designing the planned Indy-style Stutz cars that O'Donnell had mentioned in his launch speech. Few people have ever seen the designs, with most Stutz enthusiasts doubting that they ever existed outside of O'Donnell's fantasies, but when I visited Virgil Jr whilst researching this story, I saw the designs hanging on his wall. Ex had created a road-version of a Stutz Indy 500 race car, and to compete alongside it, he designed two

more, a Mercer and an unnamed Indy racer that carried Ex's stylized X motif. These cars got no further than the drawing board as Stutz concentrated on more traditional road cars.

In 1972, Ex was introduced to Californian naval architect John Noryak via a contact he had with the Duesenberg project. Noryak wanted to build a line of large fiberglass cabin cruisers, so commissioned Ex to come up with some ideas. Ex was also working on a series of paintings of great European castles, with some beautiful preliminary color sketches already completed, and consulting on further Stutz models. O'Donnell was interested in exploring different

In a press release dated January 1970, James O'Donnell stated that Stutz would build an Indy-style racer modified for street use. These designs have never been seen and Stutz enthusiasts have doubted their existence. Whilst researching this book I found the illustration for the Stutz Indy hanging on the wall of Virgil Jr's Florida home. They included not only the Stutz race car finished in red, but also designs for cars that could compete with it, including a beautiful green sportscar that could have been street legal and ready to race. It carried Exner's X motif on the head restraint. (Peter Madle)

Another race car was this pure Indy 500 vehicle that carried Exner's favorite number, 5, and a huge air spoiler.

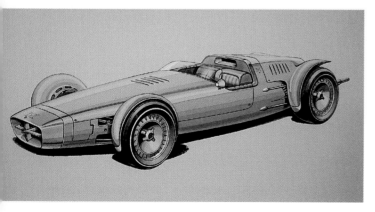

The last of the four was this light blue two-seater road-going race car. All of these vehicles had foldaway head lights built into the body. (Peter Madle)

avenues with the Stutz name and asked Ex to work on a design for a Stutz powerboat that would compliment the cars. These would be the last creative works that he would do. On 21st December 1973, Ex was rushed to the William Beaumont Hospital in Birmingham, Michigan where he died the following day from a ruptured cerebral aneurysm, with Mildred at his side.

Many close friends, family, and colleagues attended the service of remembrance at the Christ Church, Cranbrook. Mourners included Tex Colbert, Jim Zeder, Maury Baldwin, Cliff Voss, Bill Brownlie, De Soto chief engineer A E (Kim) Kimberly and his wife Louise (Louise was Mildred's best friend in Birmingham), Dr Fred and Helen Hicks, Mayor of Buchanan Joe Bachman, Bill Mitchell, Gordon Buehrig, Paul Ackerman and numerous others, filling the church. Also attending was Art Allen, the school friend that Exner had gone to the Detroit Motor Show with back in 1920 to see the Duesenberg. Virgil Jr and his wife Janet flew in from England, met by the Kimberlys, while Marie flew in from California to join Bronwen and Mildred. In a private service held a few days later, Virgil Max Exner Senior was laid to rest at St Joseph County Memorial Cemetery in South Bend, where he was reunited with his son Brian, and joined in early May 1986 by Mildred.

I recently spoke to Dana Waterman, a design engineer that has worked for some of the greats in automotive design, including Harley Earl, Bill Mitchell and Elwood Engle. He told me, "I worked for those guys, but Ex was unique, he was an artist who loved cars, but the others were sons of bitches that loved cars. They were all tough bozos that drove their designers really hard, but Ex was a great guy to work for." Bill Robinson agreed: "His

In 1972, Ex was contacted by Californian naval architect John Noryak, with a request to design a series of modern fiberglass-hulled cabin cruisers. The project went beyond the sketch stage, progressing as far as this clay model.

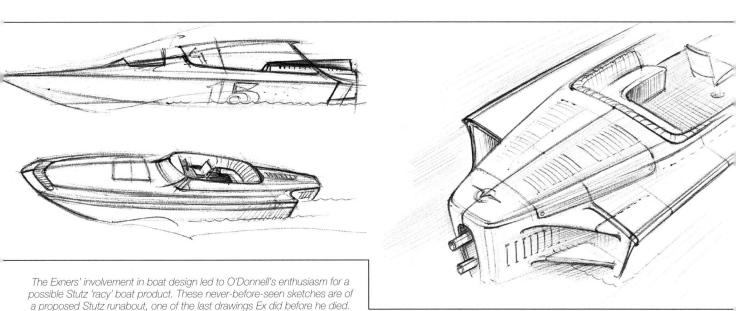

The Exners' involvement in boat design led to O'Donnell's enthusiasm for a possible Stutz 'racy' boat product. These never-before-seen sketches are of a proposed Stutz runabout, one of the last drawings Ex did before he died.

relationship with you was like a colleague, not like you was talking with a Vice President, it was two designers getting together and that's a very unique relationship to have. He would talk design with you and wouldn't put you down or put pressure on you. There were times when he came in wearing his $500 silk suits, and he had a lot of great designers working for him, but that wheel opening had to be done by him and he would get down in the clay and

This family snapshot is the last known photograph of Virgil Exner, taken alongside two Oldsmobile-Hurst 'Official Cars' at the Indy 500 in May 1972.

put that wheel opening in. He had a great deal of respect for his designers but he was a perfectionist and he wanted that control, but he was the most creative designer I ever worked with."

John Samsen worked in the De Soto studio at that time and told me, "I found Virgil to be a good man, even-tempered, with little of the eccentricities and wildness that some well-known designers showed. I considered him to be a very talented and original designer, and I shared

Virgil Max Exner Senior was laid to rest at St Joseph County Memorial Cemetery in South Bend, where he was reunited with his son, Brian, and joined in early May 1986 by Mildred.

his desire for cars to be 'pure' and automotive, making a feature of the wheels rather than hiding them; not much chrome and ornamentation, artistically sculpted bodies, etc. Exner did not want to copy the type of design other companies were producing, but was very original and creative and was not afraid to go in different directions. His design was an asset to the Studebaker Corp when they brought out the first all-new post-war car. I think that if Exner had come along in the 1990s, his design ideas would have been in the forefront of today's offerings; sculptural, aerodynamic bodies, emphasis on the wheels, minimal chrome, etc. I think he would have liked a lot of the cars on the road now." Designer Dave Cummins thinks that Ex had a real effect on car design: "Exner's real legacy and purpose was to establish a professional design section at Chrysler Corp. Another legacy that has lasted up to very recently, was a fine sense of form and shape refinement, regardless of fads or design themes. His high points are well known - most of the 'Ex era' show cars built by Ghia, and the 1957 corporate designs which heavily influenced GM from 1959 on, were a real revolt

Virgil Max Exner Sr. 24.09.1909 to 22.11.1973.

against the heavy-handed work they had done of late." To former Chrysler design executive Bill Brownlie, Exner was a "warm, personable, father-like figure, intensely interested in car design, who loved cars and hated administration. He liked to be in the studio; he was a hands-on person. You could walk into his office and discuss design with Ex. He had an intuitive sense of body form. He was concerned primarily with the side, the silhouette, proportion, and mass. He was truly the father of re-proportioning the car and the shape of the automobile. He was a visionary."

In 1990, Virgil Exner featured in the *Eyes on the Classics* when he posthumously received the Designer Lifetime Achievement Award. This was followed in 1993 when the Henry Ford Museum honoured him with its 'Lifelong Accomplishments in American Automotive Design'. Ex was also inducted into the Automotive Hall of Fame in 1995.

Virgil Exner gave the world so much more than beautiful, elegant cars; his visionary outlook molded the way vehicles would be designed and proportioned, reshaping the modern American automobile and establishing the design pattern for all modern cars. He remained modest about his achievements but he brought his own elegance and style to inanimate objects, creating art on wheels, loved the world over. No, he did not want to play the politics game, which became his undoing at Chrysler. Nor was he, or did he ever want to be, an administrative manager, but what he could do was paint, mold, and build the visions inside his mind. As well as having the admiration of his colleagues, he was also highly revered by his competitors, a rare occurrence in the automotive world. Virgil Exner was from a time when one man could be responsible for the style of a car, or a range of cars, when the designers were bold and charismatic and exerted control over the design process. So successful was he with the Studebaker Starlight Coupe, his breathtaking 'idea cars', and Forward Look production cars, he became a household name. Those days are sadly long gone. When he died in December 1973, he had so much more to give but he left behind a wonderful legacy that enthusiasts can enjoy well into the 21st century. He really was the last of the great automobile designers.

In telling the story of Virgil Exner Senior, it is hard not to digress and mention the life and career of his son, Virgil Exner Jr. As an accomplished automotive designer in his own right, their stories cross over many times, so it is far easier for me to set aside space here than to try and intertwine them through the main body of text. Virgil Jr's life could fill a whole book but here are some highlights.

He was born in South Bend, Indiana on 17th April 1933 and was the first of three children born to Mildred. Always drawing or modeling clay along with his father, it was no surprise when, in the fall of 1945, seventh grader Virgil Jr came home from school excitedly clutching an entry form for the Fisher Body competition. The Fisher Body Craftsman's Guild was a national auto design competition sponsored by the Fisher Body Division of General Motors. This competition was for teenagers to compete for college scholarships by designing and building either scale model Napoleonic coaches depicting the Fisher Body logo (1930-48), or scale model 'dream' cars (1937-68). It helped identify and nurture a whole generation of designers and design executives. He passionately pleaded to be allowed to enter, his request, of course, being granted. Unbeknownst to the twelve-year-old, his father was a great supporter of the event and had been the first judge of that same competition back in 1937 when he was head of Pontiac. Virgil made up a lot of drawings and sketches and started a 1/10-scale clay model, the wooden buck and clay having been donated by his Studebaker modeler friends and his father.

Most of his many design drawings were scrapped as he found working in three dimensions better suited to his creativity, and developed his final design directly

1937 Virgil Jr in 'Ol No 5'. Virgil Sr's favorite number was 5, and could be seen on many of his designs. This picture of Jr shows that not even the pedal cars went untouched. Junior would go on to wear the number 5 on his football and basketball jerseys through high school.

A doting son huddles up to his father and younger brother Brian on a sunny day in autumn 1940. Father and son remained close throughout their lives.

in clay. By the spring of 1946, he had cast the model in plaster from his plaster molds. With the deadline fast approaching, the cast was baked in Mildred's oven at home to speed up the process but it suffered severe cracking. With help from his father, remedial work was carried out, and then the body was sanded and painted. Chunks of aluminum were hewn into trim parts, polished, and attached. With just hours to go before the deadline, the car was ready. Virgil's entry won the junior division with an award of a $4000 scholarship that could be used to pay for education anywhere in the country. His justly proud parents sent him a telegram, reading, "We hope you will always think of today as one of the most memorable occasions in your life."

Anything automotive was of interest to the boy; he built and organized soapbox derby races for

Virgil at home in South Bend, working on his clay model for the Fisher Body competition in 1946.

The model survives to this day; testament to the quality of the build.

the local kids, even promoting the events with his own programmes, and accompanying his parents to race meetings. In 1949, the family moved from South Bend to Birmingham in Michigan so that Ex could work for Chrysler. Virgil was enrolled into Cranbrook Boys School, a private school in Bloomfield Hills,

Virgil wears the coveted winner's beret. His entry won the 1946 junior division with an award of a $4000 scholarship.

After leaving high school, Virgil followed in his father's footsteps and enrolled at Notre Dame University. This is Virgil in 1951 working on a small scale clay model.

Ex and Virgil discuss writing out another student check in Virgil's apartment at Notre Dame University in 1957. (Notre Dame University)

as a boarding pupil, even though the family home was but a few miles away. Here he became the president of the model club and won the Trinity College Award while studying. He had already decided he wanted to become an automotive designer but no organizations existed at that time that could offer a design course, so after graduating in 1951 he followed his father's footsteps and enrolled into the University of Notre Dame, the scholarship money helping to pay for his tuition. This was an exciting and important time in Junior's life. On joining the university he signed up for the Air Force's Reserve Officers' Training Corps (ROTC) while he studied Architectural Engineering for two years then switched to fine art, winning the Jacques Gold Medal of Fine Art, but it was still automotive design that he wanted pursue. Notre Dame did not have a recognized automotive design course, but over a period of

time, Virgil persuaded his professor, Frederick Beckman, that it was just what Notre Dame needed. With influence from his father and sponsorship from Chrysler, he and Beckman set up a transportation design course in 1956 with Virgil taking the position of graduate teaching fellow. From the time he took his AB degree in May of 1956 until his MA degree in August of 1957, Virgil remained a graduate student and a paid graduate teaching assistant. Ex had taken a great interest in the university, and in 1956 was made a life member of Notre Dame's Arts Advisory Council, while Mildred became a life member of their Women's Advisory Council and voted against admitting women to the university in 1973. This patronage would continue until their deaths, and for Notre Dame it was particularly useful as a way of obtaining funding from industry.

Ex was a frequent visitor to Notre Dame. Here he discusses the merits of a design with the transportation design course students. (Notre Dame University)

While teaching the design course, the younger Exner continued studying, working on a design for a Simca sportscar for his master's thesis project. In 1954, Junior had purchased a 1950 Fiat chassis from family friend Paul Farago and set about building a sportscar. He worked on the running chassis as part of his undergraduate design thesis through 1955/56 using Simca mechanical components. To go with the chassis, he wrote a paper on the project and designed and built a ¼-scale model of the intended car. This work won Virgil the highest honour award for that time, the Jacques Gold Medal of Fine Arts. By 1957, Virgil was fabricating a fiberglass body to fit around the modified rolling stock and tubular frame. The funding from Chrysler helped to pay for the conversion of the attic space of the university's Arts & Letters Building into a studio for the design course, and it was here that Junior built a full-size clay model of his intended sportscar. His intention was to cast the molds needed for the fiberglass body directly from the model, but time

was running out. With his call-up to active duty in the Air Force imminent, work was stepped up. After graduating in the fall of 1957, he left for four weeks of basic officer training at Langley Air Force Base in Virginia, then returned to South Bend. Professor Beckman had held on to the model until his return, and while teaching at the university, Junior worked on his car. To make the course he was running more interesting, he would sometimes invite designers from Chrysler, or the nearby Studebaker-Packard studio to visit and lecture. Through this contact, he made friends with some of the younger designers, which in turn led to him being hired by Duncan McCrea, a friend of his fathers and head of the design studio at Studebaker. Virgil spent six months at Studebaker from October 1957, working alongside Del Coates and Emil Bocade, contributing to McCrea's design for the 1959 Lark. In his spare time, Virgil cast his fiberglass panels for the Simca and transported them up to Detroit. He left Studebaker-Packard in February 1958 and was given a small space at the Dual-Ghia factory from Paul Farago and Gene Cassarole. With the casting finished, the panels were mounted on the car but Virgil was out of time. He had to report to Shephard Air Force Base in Texas to train as a Transportation Officer in August of that year, so he left the car in the hands of a Detroit paint bodyshop. When he returned a month later, he detailed the car and drove it back to Notre Dame to be photographed. He left for active service in Korea a few weeks later, leaving the car with friends at a sportscar shop.

The sportscar shop showed the car around, and was seen by Simca executives who wanted to use it at the 1959 Paris Auto Show, to promote the newly acquired

Talbot name. Through a phone call to Kunsan Air Force Base in Korea, Virgil agreed that Simca could use the car and so it was flown to France. On his return to the United States, he was posted to Travis Air Force Base near San Francisco for two years, and found a beautiful Fiat roadster awaiting his arrival as a thank you from Simca for using his sportscar. Virgil kept and used the Simca until he left the Air Force. It was then sold and still survives to this day, although in slightly modified form. It was while

stationed at Travis that he did contractual design work for Luigi Segre at Ghia. Renault executives had approached Ghia, wanting to emulate the success of the VW Karmann Ghia, with a car based around the Dauphine platform. Luigi Segre accepted the job and on a trip to the States he approached Ex to design the car. Because of his work with Chrysler, he turned his friend down, but did suggest Virgil Jr for the job. Virgil was given the preliminary sketches done by Renault stylists for a two-door

Virgil created a unique sportscar called the Simca Special for his master's thesis project. Built on a 1950 Fiat chassis and utilising Simca mechanical components, the body was finished in fiberglass. It had no doors; entry was by sitting on the fin and swinging one's legs into the cockpit, then lowering the one-piece bubble canopy into place. Before the body was completed, Virgil used to race the running chassis in hill climb competitions. The car is seen here outside the Exner home at 1036 Westwood Drive, Birmingham, MI, alongside Mildred's 1958 Plymouth Belvedere.

Funding from Chrysler paid for the conversion of roof space into a design center at Notre Dame. Designers from Studebaker and Chrysler often came to teach the students. (Notre Dame University)

convertible. Based on the exact parameters of the Dauphine and seeing the direction that Renault wanted to go in, he created initial sketches for Segre and sent them to Segre before leaving for Shephard AFB in 1958. The car, called the Caravelle, would evolve into the Renault Floride, and sold 49,716 units between 1959 and 1963 when production of the little convertible ceased. While in Korea, the cold weather kept Virgil from doing much design work, although he did manage to create the basic concept for the Volvo P-1800 sports coupe. On his return

Right & below: While Virgil served in Korea, the Simca was shown at various car shows, often winning trophies. When it was shown at the Henry Ford Museum's Sports Car Review, the Simca Special was seen by Simca executives. They asked if they could use it to promote the newly acquired Talbot marque, so the car was shipped to France for the 1959 Paris Auto Show, where it caused quite a stir.

This dashing young man is Virgil M Exner Jr, USAF Lieutenant. Virgil served as a transportation control officer. The photo was taken at Tachikawa Air Base in Japan in 1959.

Designed by Virgil, the 1960 Selene II was an unrealistic forward control, rear-engine configuration concept car made by Ghia. The engine-less mock-up called for the driver to clamber over the rear passengers to get to the driver's position. With its chrome cross bumper, the rear end was heavily influenced by the XNR 500. The car is still in existence.

The Exner family certainly had gasoline in its blood. Ex passed on the racing bug to his son. This is Virgil in 1965 at the wheel of his 1927 Type 40 Bugatti, at Waterford Hills, MI.

to America and still working via postal correspondence, he also designed the Karmann Ghia 1500, the futuristic Selene II show car, the Renault R-4, a Go Kart, and the FIAT 1900S Coupe that became the 2100 S, through his contract with Ghia.

In the summer of 1960, Virgil was able to take advantage of a 42-day leave pass and managed to cadge a flight across the Atlantic to Rhine Main Air Force Base in Germany on a military aircraft. He then trained to Paris to meet up with his parents and sisters for the Paris Motor Show. The Exner family rendezvoused with Paul Farago, Luigi Segre, and Segre's Brazilian born wife Luisa, and drove across Europe through Turin and Florence, down to Rome for the remainder of the vacation.

At the end of 1961, he left the Air Force with the rank of Captain and returned home to join forces with his father to create Virgil M Exner, Inc early the following year. From 1962 until he left to work for Ford, he helped his father with all of the design work including automobile design consultancy for Ghia, Pininfarina, US Steel, Duesenberg Corp, Stutz, The Copper Development Association, and Renwal Models. He also had a great deal of input on the cabin cruisers for Riva and Buhler Turbocraft. One of the

Virgil and Janet Exner stand in his study in Palm City, Florida in March 2003.

Cadillac Carrefour LX

V. M. EXNER, JR. '06

A Cadillac Carrefour LX as envisioned by Virgil and presented at the Cadillac-LaSalle Club's national meet in 2006.

designs he is most proud of was the trophy for *Motor Trend's* Car of the Year. The trophy, which depicts a set of calipers sitting on top of a round base, has been modified but is still in use today. With his marriage to Janet K Boyle in 1966, there was a need to earn some money, and with little coming into Exner, Inc, Junior decided to look for a position at one of the larger manufacturers. With Exner, Inc's reputation, Junior could almost pick which manufacturer to work for and he decided to move to Ford. For the next twenty-one years, Junior worked for that company, spending two years in Dearborn before being transferred to Ford of Germany for a year, then to Ford of England for four years. He contributed toward the 1970 Thunderbird and Maverick, the 1971 Pinto and full-size Mercury, as well as the European Escort, Granada and Fiesta.

On returning to Detroit in 1974, he worked on the 1979 Crown Victoria and Grand Marquis, and the 1980 Thunderbird before moving to the Advanced Exterior Concepts Studio, from which he retired as manager in 1988. I say retired, but I don't think automobile designers ever really retire, and since leaving Ford he has had many contemporary designs published and has been active on committees for historical cars to architecture. After having spent many years living in Palm City, Florida, Virgil and Janet reside in South Bend, Indiana, where Virgil is 'Back Home Again'.

ACKNOWLEDGMENTS

Jon Bill, archivist, Auburn Cord Duesenberg Museum
Dick Burke, Engineer
David Burgess-Wise
Jo Bortz, Bortz Collection
Geoff Carverhill, 1938 Pontiac image
Del Coates
Dave Cummins, Designer
Jon Day, Beaulieu Photographic Archives
Marie Exner
Mariella Glbellini, Riva Historical Society
Jeffrey I Godshall, Designer
David Hill, archivist, Ford UK
Richard Howes, Photographer
Shahed Hussain, *Velocity Automotive Journal*
Linda Kemp, an ace researcher
Laurence Loewy
Peter Madle, Stutz images
David Munson, 1962 Imperial
John 'Arnie' Ridley, a most generous host
Bill Robinson, Designer
John Samsen, Designer
Alberta Savonuzzi
Brett Snyder, Forward Look images
Richard Starkweather, Proof reader
Gary P Szechy, Weasel photographs
Dana Waterman, Engineer
David Welch, DUKW photograph
Kenyon Wills, imperialclub.com

My huge thanks to all of these people for their time and effort and especially Brett Snyder, who went well above and beyond the call of duty, and Rod Grainger at Veloce for taking on this project, but without the support of Virgil and Janet Exner, this book would not have seen completion. A special thank you to them, and of course, my ever-patient wife, Catherine. How does she cope with me?!

BIBLIOGRAPHY

There have been many articles on Virgil M Exner over the years; all give differing accounts of his life. Some of the better ones are listed below along with other publications that were a huge help in bringing Ex's story to print. My thanks to all of the authors.
Hyde, Charles K, *Riding The Roller Coaster*, Wayne State University Press, 2003
Flammang, James M, *The Chrysler Chronicles*, Publications International Ltd, 1994
Lee, John, *Standard Catalogue of Chrysler*, Motorbooks International, 1990
Godfrey Jeffrey I, *Opportunity Knocked*, Collectible Automobile, December 1996
Katz, John F, Profile, *Collectible Automobile,* December 1994
Lamm, Michael & Holls, David, *A Century of Automotive Style*
Burgess-Wise, David, *Ghia, Ford's Carrozzeria*, Motorbooks International 1985
Ackerson, Robert, *Chrysler 300 Series*, Veloce Publishing

Also from Veloce Publishing …

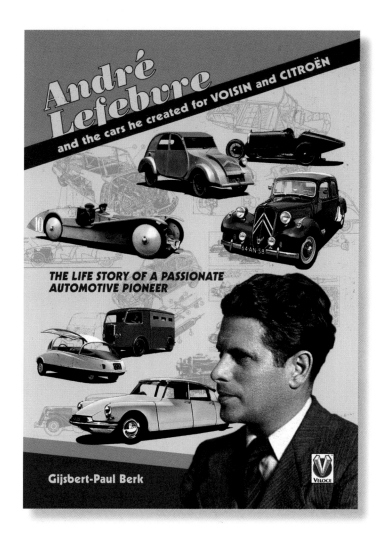

Now in paperback. This biography of André Lefebvre gives a revealing insight to the work of a practically unknown aeronautic engineer. Responsible for the minimalist 2CV and the Citroën DS – the sensation of the automotive world in 1955 – Lefebvre remains an icon of original automobile engineering and avant-garde design to this day.

ISBN: 978-1-845842-44-4
Paperback • 23.8x17cm • £19.99* UK/$34.95* USA • 144 pages • 154 colour and b&w pictures

For more info on Veloce titles, visit our website at www.veloce.co.uk
• email: info@veloce.co.uk • Tel: +44(0)1305 260068

* prices subject to change, p&p extra

Also from Veloce Publishing ...

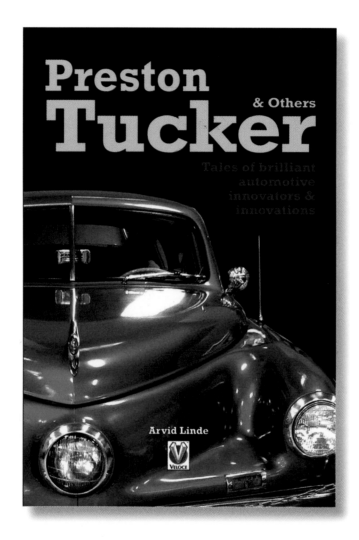

Celebrates those individuals with a radical, non-conformist approach to car design, from Preston Tucker and his Torpedo to Guy Negre and his zero-emission dream. Lavishly illustrated and intensively researched, it is also the story of the milestone inventions that have shaped today's cars.

ISBN: 978-1-845840-17-4
Paperback • 22.5x15.2cm • £19.99* UK/$39.95* USA • 160 pages • 165 colour and b&w pictures

For more info on Veloce titles, visit our website at www.veloce.co.uk
• email: info@veloce.co.uk • Tel: +44(0)1305 260068

* prices subject to change, p&p extra

Also from Veloce Publishing …

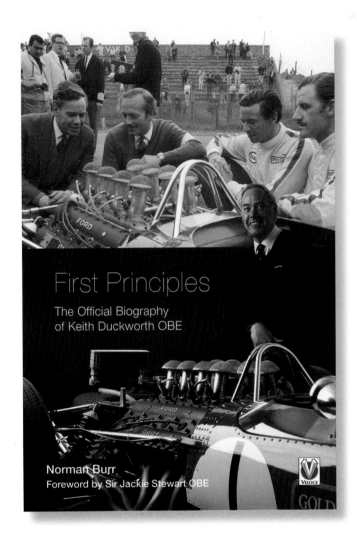

This is the story of perhaps the most talented engineer to emerge from Britain in the 20th century. Keith Duckworth's contribution to motorsport, through Cosworth Engineering, is well documented, but the story of how he arrived at that point is much less well known.

ISBN: 978-1-845845-28-5
Hardback • 23.2x15.5cm • £35* UK/$59.95* USA • 352 pages • 200 pictures

For more info on Veloce titles, visit our website at www.veloce.co.uk
• email: info@veloce.co.uk • Tel: +44(0)1305 260068

* prices subject to change, p&p extra

Also from Veloce Publishing ...

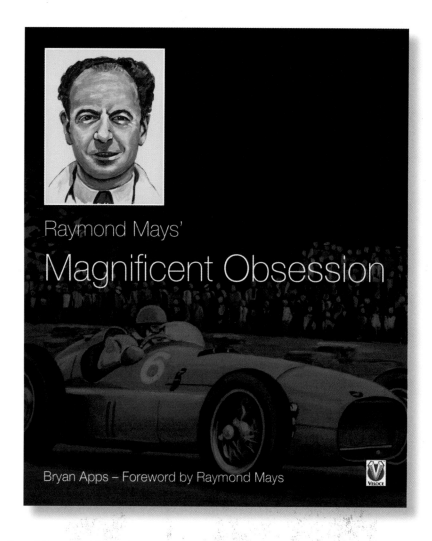

This biography of Raymond Mays includes complete histories of ERA and BRM, a foreword by Mays himself, and personal letters addressed to the author from Alfred Owen, David Brown, Tony Rudd, Rivers Fletcher, Bob Gerard, Ken Richardson, Juan Fangio, and many others, and is illustrated with over 100 of the author's paintings.

ISBN: 978-1-845847-86-9
Hardback • 25x20.7cm • £40* UK/$65* USA • 208 pages • 243 pictures

For more info on Veloce titles, visit our website at www.veloce.co.uk
• email: info@veloce.co.uk • Tel: +44(0)1305 260068

* prices subject to change, p&p extra

INDEX